The Essential Empath

complete energetic and emotional self-care

First Edition

Sarah Petruno

Dedicated to my sweet little empath baby, Cora

Contents

Introduction

Welcome!

I wrote the Essential Empath from a place of understanding and support. As a fellow empath and energy sensitive myself, I know that navigating the world as someone sensitive to emotion can, at times, be challenging and that resources on management or coping skills can be difficult to find. Understanding and having an awareness of what it means to be an empath, and having the tools available to you for managing your energetic and emotional state are integral to maintaining a steady emotional state of well-being.

Being an empath is a gift, rather than a curse. All it takes is a shift in awareness. It means that you have a deeper, immediate awareness of what another person is feeling. As such, you have the ability to shift your behavior, your reaction, and your emotional state to support and align with another. While yes, feeling the emotions of others often means that you may feel all the bad emotions, but it also means that you get to feel all the good ones, too.

In this book, you will gain the knowledge and tools needed to decide which emotions you feel and let affect you, and which ones you don't.

From a personal standpoint, I've previously undergone many treatments for anxiety, depression, and other mood disorders. I bounced from therapist to therapist and from drug to drug, and even still, my anxiety, depression, and unstable mood state remained unmanaged. I was miserable, my closest loved ones were being made miserable, and I had a host of anxiety related, physical symptoms, like upset stomach, difficulty breathing, and uncontrollable hiccupping. I was experiencing all the indicators known to empaths, with no known skills on how to manage it.

After years of seeking therapists for treatment, some helpful, some not, and countless prescriptions and dosage adjustments, I finally decided, naturally, that it was time to step away from therapy and medication. In part, I walked away because I grew tired of explaining my life to therapist after therapist, searching for the right person. And in part, because I was starting to think about having a baby and was on medications relatively incompatible with pregnancy.

Interestingly, it was not until I started developing my energetic gifts and an energetic awareness of the world around me that slowly, my anxiety, my mood disorders, and the related physical symptoms disappeared.

This is because, at the core, emotions are energy. My emotions are energy, your emotions are energy, all emotions are energy. In gaining awareness of this reality, you become aware of what emotions are yours, and what emotions aren't, and in doing so, you gain emotional stability and core well-being. You get to choose which emotions you accept and reject in order to maintain your well-being.

The Essential Empath is designed for awareness, understanding, and management of your empathic and energetic gift. As an empath, you can sense and often feel the emotions of others. You can sense and feel energy.

The Essential Empath is designed as a core tool for anyone with empathic sensitivities, abilities, or inclinations. In other words, it's designed for anyone with a sensitivity to our energetic world.

You will learn the workings of the Human Energetic System and what that means for you as an individual, operating in your surroundings and within your day to day interactions. You will learn what it means to be empathic, energetically, and you will be given the understanding needed to integrate this new found knowledge into your life. You will gain the tools, techniques, and practical knowledge necessary to manage your emotional well-being as an empath.

Informational and empowering, this books gives you the tools and practical solutions to manage, maintain, and protect your energetic and emotional self from energetic and emotional fluctuations of others, as you navigate through life. The Essential Empath is geared towards energetic understanding and management of your overall emotional well-being. Strong empathic ability is a gift, and this course, is about informed and empowered use of that gift.

With awareness, I found emotional and energetic well-being. I wrote this book so that you can find it, too.

I invite all empathic individuals and their loved ones to read and understand the material presented in this book. If you love an empath, an awareness and understanding of their gift allows you to better support, understand, and connect with them.

As you move through this book, I encourage you to pause and reflect, whenever you need, on what has been covered and what that means for your personal experience. The subject matter may be new and different from what you already know, and integrating this or any new perspective, can take time and understanding. Remember to be gentle on yourself.

Thank you for allowing me to accompany you on your journey,

Sarah

Understanding Empathy

Chapter 1

Emotions as Energy

Emotions are energy. Like two strands of DNA, emotions and energy are completely and totally, interlinked and woven together. Emotions carry with them an energetic nature, and behind each emotion, is energy supporting its existence. Energy is the support system on which emotions stand; there is no separating them. If you have no support, you have no emotional substance.

As an empath, you have the ability to sense the energy attached to the emotion. Your ability is to sense, feel, and deeply connect to the emotions and feelings of another person. You have the gift to naturally sense energy, with no special training at all. Without practicing, specializing, or even necessarily knowing what you're doing, you're an energy specialist, masked with the title of an empath.

An empath, traditionally defined, is someone with the strong trait ability to feel the emotions of another person. It's the ability to share and understand, deeply, the feelings of another. This is considered a personality trait, empathy, and as such, an unchangeable aspect of yourself.

If you are an empath, you may have been described as a too sensitive, dramatic over feeler, but you may also have been described as an understanding, compassionate and loving person. This is because you have the gift and ability to understand the emotions of another, because most often, you can feel it yourself. You know exactly what it feels like to be in another person's shoes emotionally because you can feel it too, at the same time they do.

Being an empathic individual is a gift. It means that you can show and feel more compassion, more love, and give more attention, when it is needed the most. It's as if you have a special gift of knowing, the exact right time when to lend a helping hand or a listening ear. You already know when to reach out to someone who is hurting, because you can feel it yourself, and you can feel when support is needed.

This feeling and sharing of another's emotional state is not a knowing, intelligently or with your brain. More so, it's considered an intuitive trait; **a psychic ability known as clairsentience, or clear feeling**. You know and sense feelings and emotions with your intuitive self. More specifically, this is happening at the level of energy. You are intuitive with your natural ability to sense energy, picking up on the energy attached to the emotion being felt. With this perception of energy, you feel and interpret, what this means and what emotion is being felt.

You can feel another person's emotional, and thus, energetic state. You are intuitively sensing energy, without even knowing it. You are what is called clairsentient, a clear feeler of energy.

By now, you are beginning to gain awareness that as an empathic person, you have the natural intuitive ability to sense the emotions of others through the energetic traits of the emotion. Emotions have energy and are energy, but what does that mean?

How can an emotion be energy?

Energy is the primary material by which the Universe exists. It's intangible, it's untouchable, it's relatively unseen. It exists, and we, as humans, collectively know it exists.

Energy powers homes, it generates vehicle movement, it structures friction on a roadway, it drives our physical bodies to awaken each day.

In fact, energy exists in all parts of all things that we do.

At an atomic level, particles such as nuclei, electrons, and neutrons, form vibrating and energetically buzzing atoms, atoms with valence shells, storing energy in the form of electrons. As more and more particles, atoms, and molecules cluster together, we begin to see molecular structures and compounds, forming bigger and stronger cohesive units. These structures build to eventually form larger structures that can be seen with the human eye, which is everything that we can see and touch in the physical world.

The wooden table tops of desks, the steel sheets formed into vehicles, and the plasma screens of computers and televisions, all are comprised of thousands, millions, of atoms, buzzing with energy.

And as humans, we are physical beings in the physical world, which means that we, too, are comprised of molecules and atoms, buzzing with energy. With each movement we take, each word we speak, each food particle we digest, energy transforms, from one thing to another thing. Thought transforms into speech. Muscle twitch transforms into fluid movement. Food transforms into usable amino acids and nutrients. An emotional thought or word transforms into a feeling.

In all of these cases, there is a transformation of energy. With the destruction of a French fry, as you chew and swallow, the energetic components of that French fry are not destroyed, but converted to energetic components usable by your body.

Thoughts and emotion, generated by you, also have energy. These are intangibles, just like energy itself.

Even still, we know, and we already feel this energy, without seeing it.

> *Have you ever noticed the heavy feeling associated with sadness or despair?*
>
> *Have you ever noticed the lightness, the levity, associated with joy and happiness?*
>
> *What about the jitteriness associated with nervousness and anxiety?*

These are emotions, which carry with them energy, creating this feeling in you. You're already sensing energy and aware of the feeling it evokes in you.

The key is developing an awareness of this change and identifying if it comes from outside of you. And usually, the problem of an empath is with sensing and feeling the emotions that are less than upbeat and instead are making you feel heavy, anxious, sad, upset, and nervous. It's the unexplained instability in mood, the sudden bouts of anxiety from no known source, or the internalizing of another's sadness.

As an empath with energetic and emotional sensing abilities, it is as though you are a radio tower, with a blinking red light, standing against the darkness of a vast night sky. Your radio tower is the beacon, and the receiving point of any radio signal coming from any direction, within range, across that night sky. You receive signals of varying strengths at close distances and far distances, and any distance in between. Radio signals that transmit sports broadcasts, news reports, and various musical genres, from jazz to hip-hop. All signals from any distance within your receiving range are picked up by and sensed by you.

Like a radio tower that attracts and receives signals from stations, your job is to discern the signal.

> *Is it too far for clarity?*

Is it worth playing on your radio?

What is the quality and type of signal?

Does this signal carry with it the type of sound I wish to play on my station?

In making those decisions, first, it is important to understand fully the types of signals that can be picked up and received by your radio tower. Next, comes an understanding of how exactly your tower works to attract and receive signals in the first place.

You are the radio tower, receiving and perceiving signals in the form of emotional energy.

Chapter 2

Types of Emotional Energy

The core identifier of an empath is the ability to sense, feel, and sometimes, take on the emotions of others. It's to know, often too well, exactly what another person or animal is feeling.

In sensing, feeling, and knowing the emotion of another, you are sensing, feeling, and perceiving the energy carried with the emotion felt.

Like a radio tower to the surrounding environment, you are first receiving the signal, in the form of energy, from an outside source, and attaching it to the associated broadcast. You receive the radio signal as energy, and through it, the music plays.

Energy is sensed, received, and perceived by you, and through it, emotion is felt. Signal first, then music.

The first part of being a signal receiver is understanding which types of signal translate to which types of music, in other words, **to understand which types of energy translate to which types of emotion.**

Each emotion has a different energy, and this makes sense because each emotion evokes a different feeling in us. Sadness and happiness, aside from their differing emotional states, make us feel different, in our hearts and often physically. With sadness, often comes a feeling of heaviness, and with happiness, often comes a feeling of lightness.

While these two emotions are complete opposite ends of the spectrum, we use them as examples to illustrate that there is, in fact, a spectrum of emotion.

Emotions exist along a continuous spectrum, from one extreme to another.

In this world, all things lie on a continuum. Extremes such as black and white exist, but most of the time, things lie somewhere in between, along a continuous spectrum.

There's a spectrum of light, from infrared to ultraviolet.

There's a continuum of agreement, from strongly disagree to strongly agree.

And there's a continuum of emotion from sad to happy, and from fear to love.

These examples all constitute and fall somewhere along the energy spectrum. Light consists of wavelengths and frequencies, and the wave patterns are formed and generated by energy.

Emotion is generated and formed by an underlying energy, and this spectrum of energy on which all things exist is known as many things, such as the path from:

Fear to Love

Dark to Light

Sadness to Joy

. . . and even,

Infrared to Ultraviolet

Depending on the situational factors and personal preference, this energetic spectrum on which all things lie carries a different nomenclature.

On an elemental level, this is the spectrum from **low vibrational energy to high vibrational energy.**

On one end of the spectrum, energy has a low vibration, having the lower frequency and longer wavelength, and slower moving, energetic form. The molecules sitting at this energy pattern move more slowly; they vibrate less intensely, you could even say, they sit lower to the surface. The energetic vibrational pattern is slow, undulating, waves with low peaks. The key is low vibration and slow movement.

On the other end of the spectrum, moving away low vibrational energy, is high vibrational energy. Energy of high vibration is faster moving, has a higher frequency, and shorter wavelength, overall, this energetic pattern is fast moving, with rapidly undulating waveforms with high peaks. The molecules sitting at this energetic state move more quickly, vibrate with more intensity, and tend to move up and away from the surface in their vibration. The key to this energy type is high vibration and fast movement.

As we move along this energetic spectrum, we encounter energy types holding varying levels of the qualities of low and high vibrational energy, some lower, some more moderate, and some higher.

Red light, for example, is considered on the low end, with longer wavelengths and lower frequency, and ultraviolet light, is considered higher on the spectrum, with shorter wavelengths and frequency.

In terms of emotion, at the lower end of the spectrum, reside emotions that are called **low energy emotions**. These include feelings like sadness, anger, fear, jealousy, and resentment. Low energy emotions are often called negative emotions.

At the higher end of the spectrum, reside emotions that we call **high energy emotions.** These include feelings like happiness, joy, elation, gratitude, value, and confidence. High energy emotions are often called positive emotions.

Both of these groupings, of course, contain within them emotions that fall somewhere along the higher end of the spectrum, and emotions that fall somewhere along the lower end of the spectrum. While there is no clear-cut off between what is considered high and what is considered low, there is a middle ground.

The middle ground between low and high is an area that is self-defined. Collectively, and by and large, the emotions on the low and high ends of the spectrum, are stable state and always high or always low. In the middle of the spectrum, is a group of moderate emotions, such as complacency, for example, that are easily swayed to either end of the spectrum based on context.

Thinking about this in terms of the visible light spectrum, yellow, for example, is towards the middle of the spectrum. Depending on the presence or absence of other colors, it can either be an orange-yellow, green-yellow, or mostly yellow.

As the perceiver and receiver of emotional energy, the types of energy in the form of emotion that you can sense, are broadly placed into two separate categories:

Low Energy Emotion and High Energy Emotion

You can feel these energetic emotions in yourself, and you can also feel them in others. The overarching goal as an individual is to be in a state where most of the time, you feel only high energy emotions. Those feel good, and we all want to experience states of happiness, joy, elation, and love, as much and as often as possible.

As humans, low energy emotions cannot be avoided. We live an interactive existence with the world and the universe and cannot control for all events, feelings, and emotional states existing in all individuals that we will potentially encounter. We strive, as humans, to experience these low energy emotions much less often than more desirable high energy emotions. Feeling low energy emotions like sadness, fear, anger, and anxiety, is not exactly pleasant, nor does it feel good in our hearts or bodies.

The goal state is to move to a place where we feel and exist at mostly high energy emotion, with only little intrusion from low energy emotion. As an empathic individual, this creates two requirements to reach this state:

> To ensure that you, as an individual, are always feeling high energy emotion

> and

> To buffer yourself from the emotions of those around you, who may not always be feeling high energy emotion.

This book is about maintaining a steady state in yourself, by gaining awareness of emotional energy existing in your environment. This environmental emotional energy can affect your emotional well-being, through your ability to sense this external emotion, energetically. We seek to always achieve a state of stability in high energy emotion, and as an empath, you are especially susceptible to the emotional energy of others, simply through your energetic gift alone.

This means that you can, and do already, sense and pick up on the high and the low energy emotions felt by others.

We know already, through our sheer experience existing, that high energy emotions feel good and low energy emotions feel bad, but why? Why is it that one end of the spectrum, high energy emotion, feels good to us, while the other end of the spectrum, low energy emotion, such as sadness, anxiety, nervousness, and fear, tends to make us feel unwell?

Why do low energy emotions feel bad and high energy emotions feel good?

If you've already started to ponder and ask this question, you're on the right track! Already noticing the difference in how these emotions feel to you, is noticing that you feel a difference in the energy carried by the emotion.

Recall that all emotion, as energy, exists along a spectrum often referred to as the path from Dark to Light, from Fear to Love, or from Sadness to Joy.

Lower on the spectrum, wavelengths are longer and frequencies are lower, energy and molecules are moving more slowly, you could even say, that there is more density. Because, from a chemical and physical standpoint, slower moving particles create a dense, solid state, and higher moving particles create a less dense, gaseous state.

With density, things often feel heavier. This heaviness, is what we feel when you sense a low energy emotion. And the lightness, is what we feel when we sense a high energy emotion, simply by the properties of energy held by the emotion. Inherently, feeling heavy or light, creates a sense of good or bad, but there's also another reason compounding on this fact.

As creatures of this Universe, we are inherently part of the Universal purpose and goal for all, the desire for universal love, respect, and compassion for ourselves and others. Universal Love. Some call this world peace, others call this enlightenment, and still others call this living in the Light.

For this universal state of being to occur, the state in which we can experience and receive universal love, we must align ourselves with the energetic frequency of this state. In other words, we can't experience the high energy state of universal love if we reside presently with or at low energy. This state creates an energetic disharmony, a discord as we experience a state that is in direct contrast with the desired goal of universal love.

Even if this state is only transitory or temporary, a disharmony with the universal goal has been reached and created. The unpleasant feeling you experience is the feeling of discomfort that arises when any disharmony is experienced.

Imagine if you went to see a concert at a local symphony hall. As you sat in the audience, and listened to the beautiful, harmonious music being created, suddenly, you noticed and heard a small disharmony, a note being played out of tune and not in harmony with the other instruments. In feeling, and hearing this disharmony, you may notice it and focus on it, and you may begin to feel uncomfortable in your seat. The bigger the clash or discord created, the more the sound creates a feeling of nails on the chalkboard. There was a moment of disharmony with one instrument and the rest of the orchestra, creating a sensation of discomfort in you.

Sound is also energy, and the brief creation of a disharmonic state was sensed and picked up by you.

When you sense and feel a low energy state coming from within yourself, or from outside of yourself in another person, you become aware of the discord. This discord, in conjunction with the energetic properties of the emotion itself, combines to create the feeling of low energy discomfort.

Low energy feels bad because of its heavy density, and it creates a discord with the universal goal of high energy love and compassion. High energy feels good because it's lighter with a lack of density and is in alignment with the universal goal of love and compassion.

With awareness and understanding of how different types of emotional energies feel, in general, now is the time to get an idea of what, specifically, these types of emotional energies feel like for you.

Chapter 2 Exercise.
Energetic Discernment of Low and High Energy

At this point in your life, or at any point past infancy and early childhood, you've already been in countless situations in which you've perceived an emotion, energetically and consciously. You've known when someone felt a certain way, just by the feeling that they were giving you.

Have you ever walked into a room with someone else, and felt a heavy sadness in the air, even with no exchange of words or obvious emoting?

Have you ever felt the happiness and joy in the presence of a child celebrating their birthday?

Have you ever been to a wedding where you could feel the love filling the room?

These are all scenarios in which you have felt emotion, where your empathy has been strongest, and in which you have sensed these emotions through associated transmission of energetic resonance.

In this exercise, you will be purposefully practicing sensing emotions as energy. Specifically, as you navigate through your day, start paying attention to the feeling an emotion gives you. Begin to pick up on sensations in your body, your mood, your behavior, your demeanor. As soon as you notice that someone around you is experiencing or did experience a particular emotion, practice identifying how that has affected you.

For example, you went to the store and the individual ahead of you in line was being particularly hostile and nasty. Later, you noticed a mood and disposition change in yourself, such that you were now feeling irritated, jittery, and hostile. This is an example in which you sensed, received, and then took on the emotional energy of another person.

In another example, let's say that someone you love got offered the job of their dreams or was just accepted into their dream college. In sharing with them their joy and elation, notice how this has changed your mood, disposition, and attitude. Do you feel better than before? Lighter? Happier? In a more uplifted mood state?

For one hour a day, three days a week, intend and decide that during that hour, you are going to be on alert for energetic shifts in yourself attributed to your interactions. Choose your hour during a time when you might find yourself interacting with others, even peripherally, like shopping in a store. Try to be diverse in your choices, selecting a variety of places and situations in which you practice. Notice shifts you experience that are to low energy, and those that are to high energy.

Begin to gain an awareness of what these shifts feel like to you personally, and how the shift manifests for you.

If you would like, keep a journal or log of the changes you notice, and soon you will have a record of which emotion creates which change in you.

If a friend was sad, how did your mood change later, if at all? Did you feel a heaviness move with you throughout the day?

If you played with a happy child, did you feel better, and lighter, afterward?

If you encountered a hostile driver, did you later feel hostile and irritable?

Take note of the changes you see in your mood, behavior, and physical sensations as you maintain awareness of your emotional shifts, and start to put the pieces together on how you are affected by the energetic shifts in others. You will soon begin to notice that many emotions, feelings, and mood states you have experienced have not been entirely due to your own causing, but rather, have arisen from your interactions with others.

As an empath, you are particularly adept in sensing, perceiving, and receiving the emotional energy of others, what is known as sharing and understanding, from a psychological standpoint. To begin managing your gift, the first and most integral step, is awareness and becoming aware of what energetic and emotional shifts come from within yourself, and which come from outside of yourself. The key is discerning where the energy comes from and what it feels like, and in doing that, you gain awareness of what emotion is yours, what isn't.

Once those distinctions are made, you can begin to create a stable state for yourself, by identifying other emotions and deciding, if you wish to allow this outside emotional and energetic change to affect your being. You can start to ask yourself:

> *Which emotional energy do I like the feeling of?*
>
> *Which emotional energy makes me feel bad?*
>
> *How does this emotional energy, right now, make me feel and do I want to remain in this state or do I want to move away from it?*

In practicing discernment, you'll begin to get a feel for the decisions you can make and in what direction you might choose. And in the following two sections, you'll learn the tools you need to actively make those choices.

As an empath, your ability is to receive, sense, and perceive the emotion of others in the form of energy. You are a radio tower and the signals sensed and perceived by you, are generated by all things in the vicinity that generate a signal, all things that generate energy to send out into the world.

And as we've covered, this is everyone and everything near you, yourself included.

You can sense emotional energy, because, on a core level, you are made up of energy. Your energetic components connect with those of another, in your daily interactions, creating an energetic connection. Similarly, when you shake hands with another person, you create physical connection between two parties. This interactive exchange and connection also happens at the level of energy, through what is called your Energetic Body.

Chapter 3

The Human Energetic Body

As a human with a physical body, you are comprised of millions of molecules. In various types and forms, these molecules combine in a variety of ways to form the complete physical structure that makes up your physical body.

These molecules, your bodily processes, and your being, are all comprised of energy. Energetic transformation and change are processes that keep you alive - from the molecules on an atomic level, and from energetic processes that occur in your body to keep you a breathing, thinking, functioning human being.

In high school biology, you may have learned of metabolic processes that occur to break down food and resources into usable metabolic energy. Energy is continually being converted and transformed, to carry out all of your physical activities.

Individual muscle contractions are together combined to form a fluid movement. This is an energetic transformation, of one thing to another thing.

Food particles are broken down into molecules carrying energetic resources through the bloodstream to all areas of your body, allowing for continual life. This is a transformation of one form of energy, food, to another form of energy, organ function, for example.

Even within the psychological mind, transformation of energy occurs. Thoughts and emotions are products of neuronal firings, through synaptic junctions, and triggering the release of hormones and other biomodulators. This is a transformation. Thinking, perceiving, and the beginnings of emotion occur within the brain, and these processes are often translated to physical functions. Neuronal firing triggers a series of downstream processes to generate an emotional response: one type of energy to another type of energy.

Your body is not only made up of energy, but it is a collective of dynamic, constantly changing, energetic transformation.

These energetic properties and functions create an entire body of energy, referred to as the **Human Energetic Body.**

This body is inherently interlinked and connected to your physical system. It's comprised an entire energetic field, created by the collective of these energetic components and processes. Your energetic body is also comprised of a series of energetic centers of concentrated energy within a system.

In the intuitive sciences, these are referred to as:

The Aura (the energy field) and the Chakras (the energetic centers)

You have an energetic body, and so does everyone else. We all have one; it's the nature of the properties of the Universe. All things are composed of *energy*: that which is never created or destroyed, only transformed.

It is through your energetic body that emotions are created first, and then emotions are manifested in your physical body and mind as feelings and sensations.

Emotions as energy reside primarily in your energetic body. In our example of you as a radio receiver tower, the tower is your energetic body.

Because other people also have energetic bodies, and you are an individual in an interactive world, your gift of empathy is active when you sense and perceive the energetic body of another. You sense, receive, and perceive their emotional energetic body. As a being capable of energetic transformation, it is often the case that the energy coming from another person's energetic body is picked up by you and transformed into a physical mind and body feeling of emotion.

On an energetic level, this is what is happening in empathy.

Energetic fields and bodies are not bound by physical density and structures, and can expand and contract. Meaning that your energetic body and the energetic body of another can easily interact and an energetic transformation, on either part, can occur.

For example, if you find yourself in the grocery store in the same aisle with a frazzled mother and a screaming child, they may carry an emotional energy of stress, nervousness, irritation, and frustration. With you in the same aisle, it's very likely that your energetic body and their combined energetic body interact. An energetic transformation occurs that takes her emotional energy into your energetic being, and as such, creating a physical feeling and sensation of irritability in you.

This energetic sharing is the core basis of empathy; your ability to share and feel the emotions of another. You are now sharing the emotional energy of the mother that was once not present in you, and once this energy is integrated into your being, you can likely feel it too.

Your energetic body is comprised of an overall energy field, the Aura, and individual concentrated centers of energy, called the chakra system.

These are the systems that act to sense, perceive, and receive the emotional energy of others. These combine to form your radio tower, which receives signals from other towers.

In the following chapters, you'll learn exercises and techniques that allow you to manage inputs to these systems and regulate emotional energy received by your energetic body. You'll learn how to create and maintain a sense of internal stability and peace to your energetic system, but first, let's briefly review the nature of these two components of your energetic body.

The Aura

The aura constitutes the exterior of your energetic body and is the equivalent of your skin and the exterior of your physical body. It is your entire energetic field, comprised of the energetic resonance of all parts that make you, you. It contains all energetic components, functions, transformations, and residual energy that exists within and around your physical body.

All parts of your body and your mind are made of and comprised of energy. All physical structures, like organs, blood, skin, bones, eyes, hair, nails, all consist of molecular structures that carry with and through them an energy. All thoughts, knowledge, emotions, feelings, ideas, and experiences are also comprised of energy. They are stored in your brain as discrete and continuous components and transformed in your mind through neuronal firing, each having a current energetic state and having the ability to transform into a new energetic state.

As energy possessed and held by your being, it creates a unique to you energetic field, which consists of all parts of you, physical and non-physical.

Bones and emotions.

Blood and sweat.

Feelings and tears.

All are energy and have energy. And anything with energy has an energetic field. This field is your aura.

The human aura exists in the shape of a large oval or egg, all around your physical body. It exists above and below you, to the back and the front of you and also through you. Imagine if you stepped into a giant, oval bubble, this is your aura.

While your aura can expand and contract to any distance near and far to your physical body, it typically lies at anywhere from 2 inches to 6 feet away from your body, in all directions.

Because of the aura's ability to expand and contract, when you go out into the world, your aura can brush up against or overlap with the auras of others. If you imagine a Venn diagram, where two circles overlap to create a gray, shaded area, this is what it looks like when auras overlap. Depending on your proximity to other people and the amount of people present, your aura could potentially overlap with many, many other auras. All the while, interacting with, sensing, and perceiving the emotional energy of everyone else.

This is where empaths run into trouble. Always sensing and perceiving the emotional energy of all others, through energetic interactions such as this, can overwhelm the system. Energetically, it's as though you are never resting or sleeping. Always scanning the horizon for potential predators and threats is tiring and, with no rest, becomes stressful and extremely overwhelming.

It's no accident that aura interaction and overlap occurs, in which you are picking up on and potentially taking on the energetic, emotional states of others. This is and was an evolutionary necessity.

As a human evolving in an unpredictable world, always needing to scan the area for threats or resources was a requirement for survival. This scanning happened in a physical sense, with your eyes and physical senses, but also with your energetic senses.

In fact, having the ability to sense and know what another individual was feeling was considered a skilled gift, in the not too distant past.

Ever wonder why one or two people were deemed the village communicators, negotiating with neighboring villages and peoples?

Or why particular individuals were chosen for conflict mediation?

The reason for this is that these individuals were extremely adept at reading the emotional and psychological state of other people and villages as a whole. They were skilled at perceiving and sensing the emotional energy, and reacting accordingly. Changing their behavior, tone, words, and speech, to best accommodate the emotional state of others. This ability is considered a skill and a gift, even today.

Now, your energetic body and physical bodies still exist with little evolutionary adaptations from this time in the past. Except now, our environment is vastly different.

There's been little change to the energetic sensory system, and lots of change to the environment in which you are sensing emotional energy.

The globe is far more populated, we live in densely packed cities and have shopping centers and towns that are concentrated with people. Our threats and needs for survival are often less pressing and urgent, but, we still have an energetic system that acts to perceive, receive, and sense the energy of others.

There's a lot more emotional energy available to sense now, simply because there's a lot more people situated closer together.

This means that depending on the day and where you live, your aura is potentially interacting and overlapping with thousands of other auras in a single day.

Your energetic body is sensing and perceiving information from potentially thousands of other individuals in a single day.

This is enough to exhaust a system and create feelings of stress and overwhelm, on top of the emotional energy present in the auras that you have interacted with.

Nowadays, there are two things going on:

Overwhelm and exhaustion from an always actively sensing energetic body.

and

Emotional, energetic inputs and transformation from the auras of others.

Being an empath means that your energetic sensitivities are stronger than others. You have a better ability, naturally, to sense, perceive, and interpret the energetic state of another person, to read their aura, and know and feel, exactly what they feel.

This is a positive evolutionary adaptation, in favor of survival, from an interpersonal sense.

Let's say, you lived in a village hundreds of years ago, and village superiors were aware of an impending threat and for whatever reason, were not sharing it with the village as a whole. As an empath with superior energetic skills, you would already know that there was a threat and be able to act accordingly.

In another example, perhaps you were negotiating terms with a hostile opponent. A very sensitive topic, and the wrong words or the wrong behavior could risk survival. As an empath, you have the superior gift of already knowing the emotional state of the other party, and can naturally, without thinking, shift your behavior and response.

Today, threats to survival like this are lower, but still exist in some cases. Most of the time, your gift of empathy is used to relate to others. Through overlapping energetic bodies, auras, you already know and can feel what someone else is feeling. As such, you can change your words, your behavior, and your response to appropriately and compassionately act.

While not necessarily survival related, this is still a gift.

Have you ever experienced a sensitive emotional state, be it sadness or joy, and interacted with someone who exactly knew what you were feeling and was able to share that moment with you, honestly?

This interaction is a gift.

The ability to connect with another person in the exact way that they need it, at any time, is a treasure, and this is the natural ability that you possess.

Your aura is the broad scale energetic system. It's the entire picture; it's all the energy combined. It's the first line of defense and protection between you and the world, similar to the skin on your physical body.

Your aura is the energetic field of all energetic components and processes contained within your being. This is the primary interaction point between yourself and others, especially if you aren't speaking or interacting, and rather, just crossing paths. The connecting and crossing of two auras is much like simply brushing past another person as you pass.

Except, in the case of the aura, there is often an energetic transfer that occurs, between your aura and the aura of another person.

Imagine if you, completely showered and clean, decided to walk through a crowd at a three-day music festival, the kind with no showers and camping only. Exactly. You'd get a little (or a lot) of grime on your skin.

But, because people tend to shower regularly, and you are not often in that close of proximity with others, this transfer of dirt from skin to skin does not often happen though it can.

Consider now that even disease is transmitted, usually unseen, through passing contact of another. When people are sick, knowingly or unknowingly, they can communicate disease to passing strangers, depending on method of transmission.

This is similar to auric transfer of energy, usually unseen and unknown by either party, two auras overlap and energy is shared between the two parties. Sometimes it's low energy; sometimes it's high energy. Sometimes you encounter people feeling happiness and joy, and sometimes you encounter people feeling sadness and despair.

Without awareness or management of this interaction, which is possible, both parties experience some level of change, energetically, to their energetic body. The degree of change depends on their degree of energy sensitivity, their degree of openness to receiving other energy and their level of proactive management. On some level, there is often an energetic transfer, and subsequently, a transformation occurs that allows you to feel and sense, the emotional energy of another person, even if you'd rather not.

The aura is part of your external energetic body that houses within it, your centralized energetic system, the chakra system. Similar to the physical body that holds within it your organs and internal functions, the aura is exterior, but it is also connecting and interacting with your inner energetic body.

Your physical body is not simply a shell that sits around your internal structures; it's an exterior and also an interior, to which internal functions and processes are connected and interacting.

Your aura sits outside your physical body like a giant bubble, as a field of energy. It is a sphere of energy, encompassing the entire body. It's not only an exterior bubble; it's an energetic field, concentrated at the middle and expanding outward becoming less concentrated as you get further away from the centralized interior. There's an outside surface, your auric skin, and there's also an interior connected to your internally housed energetic system, the chakra system.

The Chakra System

The chakra system is your internal, centralized energetic system as part of your overall energetic body. Your aura is the peripheral, generalized system, and your chakra system is the centralized, specified system.

We can liken these two systems to your peripheral and centralized nervous system. The peripheral nervous system provides a non-specific response while the centralized nervous system provides a more specific response to environmental, psychological, and physiological changes and stressors.

The aura is your first defense and protective layer to the world and is the first recipient and sensory system of any emotional energy you should come in contact with. It's a peripheral system linked to a central system, the chakras.

A chakra itself is an energetic center, an area of concentrated, swirling energy. We can think of these as mini-subenergetic fields, areas where energetic components are densely packed, and as such, create small energetic centers themselves.

There are thousands of chakras throughout the body, which are completely circular in shape when functioning optimally, and these are your centralized energetic response systems.

Where the aura is your peripheral non-specific energy sensing system, your chakras are your centralized specific energy sensing systems.

Using the physical body as an example, imagine that your hand touches a hot stove burner. You have a peripheral sensory system in your hands that creates a reactive impulse to immediately retract your hand. Soon after, the peripheral nerve endings in your finger send a signal to your brain, your central nervous system, about the incident, and your brain responds by producing the feeling of pain, appropriately. The peripheral response is to move away, and the central response generates a feeling of pain.

With the chakra system and the aura, the systems are similarly connected. With your aura, you receive an immediate perception and an idea about a person or situation, and once that information is transmitted to your chakra system, an appropriate response is formed.

While there are many, many energy centers, there are seven major energy centers, known as the seven primary chakras. Each chakra has a specific function and associated physical, mental, and emotional systems.

The 7 Chakras

The seven primary chakras begin at the bottom of your feet and move all the way up to the top of your head, they are:

- Root Chakra
- Sacral Chakra
- Solar Plexus Chakra
- Heart Chakra
- Throat Chakra
- Third Eye Chakra

- Crown Chakra

In and of themselves, each of these chakras are responsible for governing not only one area of the body, but also their corresponding emotional areas and many physiological and physical systems.

The chakra system is linked to events occurring in our emotional life, our physical life, and our physiological life. Each chakra, each energetic center, has a corresponding system within the central energetic body.

The chakras are in charge of creating a coordinated specific response to events in our life while the aura responds more generally.

Imagine that you were insulted by a stranger in the store, or you overheard a personally offensive comment. Your peripheral, auric response is repulsion and feeling the need to move away. Your chakra specific response, depending on the nature of the comment, is to feel a blow to your self-confidence (your solar plexus chakra), or a hurt in your heart (your heart chakra).

While these are examples of chakra specific effects, as an empath, it's less important to focus on the specific function of each chakra. Rather, we focus on the changes and processes of your entire energetic system as a whole. The sensations you feel, when you sense emotion, are the result of an entire energetic body functioning together with your physical body[1].

When your aura senses and receives an energetic input and subsequent change in your energy field, it is your chakra system, in conjunction with your physical and physiological systems, that creates a specific response. All systems function together to generate a response.

---

[1] While the chakra system and working within it is important, in this book, we will focus on more overarching tools and concepts, less so on specific chakras.

The aura and the chakra system combine to form your complete energetic body. Your physical body and your energetic body are inherently linked, with a change in one, seeing a change in the other. As an empathic individual, it is your energetic system sensing a change in and interacting with, the energetic systems of others.

Your energetic system communicates and relays information to your physical system, generating a physical feeling of emotion and a physical response, such as the feeling of heaviness with sadness and the physical production of tears. This emotional energetic information was received and perceived by your energetic system and translated into a tangible, physical sensation. In another example, let's say that you are presenting your work at a large scale conference. Before you arrive at the conference hall, you're feeling pretty calm. You know your presentation and topic well, and there are minimal, if any, feelings of nervousness or anxiety, until, that is, you enter into the conference center.

As a physical and energetic individual, you enter into the building, and you can immediately look around the room, feel the cool of the air conditioning on your skin, and hear people practicing their talks. You're using your physical senses to interpret the scene. On the other hand, you also have that energetic body. Your aura, first, is interacting with the energy fields of all others in that space that have an energetic field. You are now potentially sharing energy with everyone else who is about to present their work, as well as the attendees.

Empathically and energetically, you are now sharing energy and emotion with others. Soon, and as the presentation grows near, you realize that your once calm and confident self has been replaced with someone who is feeling anxiety, nerves, and doubt in self-confidence. You stomach may even have butterflies now.

And guess what! You just underwent a change to your energetic body. Your aura, or energy field, sensed, received, and interpreted the energetic, emotional content of the other nervous auras in the room. Then, because the emotion related to feelings of confidence, an area governed by the solar plexus chakra, or the stomach chakra, you started to feel a physical manifestation of the nervousness in your stomach.

Your peripheral nervous system, your aura, sensed and received, and sent information to the appropriate centralized system, the solar plexus chakra, and you experienced a change in emotional and physical state.
You shared the emotion, and as such, energy with others. In this way, you felt and understood the emotion of others in a situation where you may not have wanted to.

There are times when this reactionary chain is beneficial as in the presence of love at a wedding, who doesn't enjoy sharing and feeling the love present in that moment?

Or, when your child gets accepted into college. It's an amazing gift to be able to share, understand, and join in feeling his elation and joy.

As an empath, your ability to sense the emotional energy of others spans the entire spectrum, from low to high energy. You have the ability to share and feel it all, just by being you.

The natural transfer of energy that occurs in your aura, the centralized response, and the physical sensation of feeling, is more heightened in you simply because you're evolutionarily more sensitive. You're more aware of emotional energy in general.

It is true that this is an inborn trait. It's an evolutionary adaptation, survival of the fittest, and you, are the fittest at understanding, feeling, and sharing emotion. It's an energetic gift and an emotional one.

Due to our current environmental state of overpopulation and more concentrated living centers, there's just more emotional energy to be aware of now.

And luckily, you get to decide when you are sensing and feeling emotional energy of others, and which emotional energy you accept into your energetic and physical body, and which emotional energy you can reject. This is an option.

You don't have to travel about this world always feeling the emotions of others, and you certainly don't have to always take them on. The only emotional energy you are in charge of handling is your own; all other emotional energy sent your way either intentionally or unintentionally, can be turned away or ignored.

An empath has the unique ability to share, feel, and understand the emotions of others. You have the ability, naturally, to sense and interpret emotional energy. This gift allows you to react more fluidly to your environment and your interactions with others. Through sensing the emotions that others are experiencing, you can perceive their emotional state. You can then shift your speech, your body language, your response, and your overall behavior to fit the needs of others and yourself, in the interaction.

You know, inherently, when to be more loving, and when you guard yourself instead. This allows you to function cohesively and cooperatively with others; it allows you to be a superior support system to your friends and family, as you always know exactly how another person is feeling. You are an expert understander, feeler, and sharer with others, and through this, others find support in you and look to you, often, for your interpretation and take on a situation.

You're likely a great read of character and excellent at seeing a person and a situation in the purest, clearest, and most honest way. No emotional filtering masks the scene because you can easily perceive it yourself.

Being an empath has many benefits, though, if you're reading this book at all, you know that it also has some pitfalls.

You can sense all emotional energy, good and bad, low energy emotion and high energy emotion. You can read others and your environment for whatever information it contains and through that perception of emotional energy, make decisions. Your energetic system is always in scan mode, sensing your environment and receiving information. It's as though your radio tower is always turned on and open to receiving a signal, whatever that signal may be.

Always alert, always interpreting, and always transforming energy from the energy received, to the energy integrated and manifested in your system.

Through this book, you will learn the tools you need to proactively manage your emotional and energetic well-being. You will learn how to release and remove emotional energy that is not welcomed by you. You will learn how to actively decide which emotional energy you wish to share with others and which emotional energy you wish to push away and reject. You will learn both strategies in preparative awareness and on the spot techniques for maintaining your emotional boundaries and sense of peace.

In the next section, *The Empath's Toolkit*, we will focus on the core management techniques for managing your energetic body, your radio tower. You will learn general procedures to prevent and enhance your always alert system from undergoing too much wear and tear. You will learn how to turn down your sensing abilities for a time and how to decisively reject or accept emotional energetic signals from others.

The Empath's Toolkit

Chapter 4

Introduction to the Toolkit

As an empath, you have the natural ability to feel, share, and understand the emotions of others. While everyone is with an energetic body, and thus, has the ability on some level to sense, feel, and perceive emotional energy, your ability is naturally stronger.

It's an inborn trait, and just as we all have natural talents, strengths, and even weakness, one of your strengths happens to be the gift of empathy.

Empathy tends to be seen and presented as negative trait, and a pitfall to your personality, often accompanied by ideas of a decreased quality of life. The gift of empathy is largely seen as not a gift at all, and rather, a plight. Even the individuals in the lives of empaths may say things like,

You're too sensitive.

You're too emotional.

Why are you so moody all the time?

Pull it together and stop crying.

The lack of understanding and availability of management practices runs so deep that many empaths are given medical diagnoses of mood disorders and instabilities.

Being an empath is often presented as a disease and a curse.

And it just isn't.

The ability to sense emotional energy more strongly than others has pluses and minuses, just like all traits, characteristics, and abilities.

If you're a naturally gifted sprinter, you will win races and excel in track and field, but you may also have muscular thighs and have difficulty finding pants that fit.

If you're naturally gifted at math, you'll excel in school and analytical fields, but you may also be teased for your enjoyment and advanced ability in math.

If you are born with the ability to hear a wider spectrum of sound, you'll be able to hear birdsong more acutely, but you may also hear unpleasant tones normally out of range of human hearing.

You were born onto this earth with the natural ability to sense more deeply, to perceive more clearly, and to share more fully in the emotions with others.

The human spectrum of emotion spans from low energy emotions, such as fear and anxiety, to high energy emotions, like love and compassion. You can sense, feel, and perceive all of it, without discrimination.

You have the ability to sense, feel, and perceive the low energy emotions of others, and you *also* have the ability to sense, feel, and perceive the high energy emotions of others.

At all times, should you so choose, you have the ability to share a unique view of another human's experience, the only closer view existing is that of the individual himself. You can feel it, you can share in it, and you can understand it exactly because it is so easily transferred and sensed by you.

Humans experience the entire gamut of emotion.

There will be times where you, as an empath, will be in the presence of someone experiencing sadness or fear, and you will be able to feel it. But with just as much frequency, you have the opportunity to be in the presence of someone experiencing happiness, love, and joy, and you have the ability to share in this feeling with them.

Through this gift, you are provided with a complex and unique view of the emotional state of another person. This allows you to respond and react accordingly.

From an evolutionary viewpoint, this makes sense. If you were in the presence of someone feeling fear from a charging bull, it would be in the best interest of your survival to also feel that same fear and react accordingly.

If you unknowingly walked into a room where everyone was experiencing grief from the loss of the loved one, it would be in your best interest to be able to sense this emotion, and react accordingly.

Even beyond a survival and social graces sense, isn't it wonderful to experience and share fully, in the happiness and joy of another? To be fully present and to feel the love, after a birth or during a wedding? To be filled with joy when watching a child laugh and play?

The ability to appreciate and experience fully with others the range of human emotion is one of the beauties of our existence on this earth. You have been given the extra boost. The insider's look. The secret key. You have the ability to tap into this magic even deeper. To love more fully, to experience more deeply, and to support more completely.

This is the gift that you have.

With this ability, you also have the ability to decide when to use it and when to turn it down. It's just a matter of learning how to use this ability and putting it to practical use, which you will learn how to do in this and the next section.

After all, we're not always in a situation where we want to be sharing in the human emotional experience. Sometimes, we just want to buy some apples and get out of the store without feeling the emotions of other shoppers.

This is a possible reality, and through learning techniques of energetic management, you can pick and choose, when, where, and what emotional energy you sense, and what emotional energy you choose to ignore.

The techniques introduced in *The Empath's Toolkit* can be grouped into three categories of energetic tools:

- **Clearing and Releasing (Chapter 5):** Removing non-you emotional energy from your field

- **Aura Expansion and Contraction (Chapter 6):** Controlling your energy field to modulate and fine tune your degree of energy sensing

- **Intentional Acceptance and Refusal (Chapter 7):** Actively deciding to accept or reject different types of emotional energy in your space

In the following chapters, we will move from core energetic technique to more advanced, from more broad spectrum, to more directed and specific.

For example, clearing and releasing is ideally a practice to be incorporated into your daily evening routine, while you may only find yourself intentionally refusing emotional energy in very directed, in the moment type situations.

While moving through the following chapters and practicing each technique, we encourage that you become familiar and comfortable with an individual practice or technique before moving on to the next. Gain mastery in one area first, before moving on to gain mastery in another.

You are certainly welcome to take archery, ballet, and horseback riding classes all at the same time. However, it may be more beneficial if you instead decide to focus your weekly practice on one thing, strengthening and developing that, before moving on to the next practice. Over time, with mastery in each area, you'll be able to easily shoot a bow and arrow while riding a horse, but it's less overwhelming to learn each skill individually at first.

Meaning, once you complete this book and practice the skills inside, you'll be able to easily contract your aura while intentionally refusing emotional energy. But first, I recommend that you learn one thing at a time, before combining tools and techniques.

In addition to the difficulty of juggling many new skills, it's important to practice each skill individually. This way, you can clearly notice and identify the changes you see from just that one change in your daily practice. If you're doing all things at once, it may be difficult to pinpoint which thing, individually or combined, was the factor causing your beneficial outcome. But, if you focus on using and practicing one skill at a time, you will know that the changes you see are due to this particular practice and nothing else.

Think of it as an experiment, if you have too many manipulated variables and not enough control, you don't know which thing caused the change in your observed variable. Whereas if you only have one manipulation, or change, while everything else remains the same, you can say with relative certainty that this one manipulated variable is the cause for the result.

You are the scientist here, manipulating your energetic well-being with the intention to achieve your desired result. It is important that you remain observant and perceptive of the changes you experience.

If you can keep the equivalent of a lab notebook, notating what change you made and what effect you saw, great. If you simply prefer to observe and take it all in intuitively, also great.

As you learn and become comfortable with managing your emotional energetic being you will gain more and more experimental observations of the changes underway and enacted by you. I encourage you to combine and experiment with each technique in differing situations and circumstances.

In assembling and familiarizing yourself with your Empath Toolkit, you will become skilled at using the tools to manipulate and master your environment. With this mastery, you can turn your emotional experience in the world into exactly what you want it to be, one of stability, peace, and happiness.

Beginning at the very first step in emotional energy management, is the act of clearing and releasing. As an individual with an energetic body, you are continually interacting with and brushing past other individuals with energetic bodies. There's bound to be some transfer of emotional energy, and, in fact, this is where most of it occurs.

Not in your individual interactions with others, but in your passing interactions.

You pass by far more individuals in your day than you ever directly interact with, and in doing so, your auras, your energy fields, cross. Emotional energy and otherwise is transferred between your auras, and is shared, and often felt, by you. Your energetic body is transferring emotional energy to and from other energetic bodies all day long. Energy is shared, received, transferred, and perceived, all just by getting out of your bed and placing yourself in an environment with other humans, in person or at a distance.

This continual contact with other energetic bodies and emotional energies takes its toll on you. When you are always alert, receiving, and perceiving emotional information in the form of energy, by the end of your day, your energy field contains a lot of emotional energy that does not belong to you. Instead, it belongs to the individuals whom you have interacted with that day, on any level.

This is where the need for clearing and releasing comes in, as it is the act of removing, releasing, and rinsing clean your energetic body.

Chapter 5

Clearing and Releasing

Clearing and releasing is like taking a shower for your energetic body.

Imagine that you were out and about all day, running errands in crowded markets, taking public transportation, visiting busy offices, traveling past dusty construction sites, and sweating in the hot sun. By the end of the day, when you finally walk into your front door, you might feel pretty dirty. You might even notice dirt and grime on your skin from sweat, from smog, from dust, and from all the surfaces and environmental pollution that has graced your skin while exposed to the elements.

After a day like this, you might feel the need to shower, to rinse yourself clean from the grime and climb into bed ready to awaken to start a fresh new day. This is the process of clearing and releasing substances from your physical body, and you can do the same for your energetic body.

The process of cleansing and releasing is the process of removing from yourself all of the emotional pollution that has attached itself to you during your day.

In your daily interactions, you are coming into contact with individuals experiencing all types of emotional energy, and through the contact of your energetic field with theirs, a transfer of energy can occur. Such that some of their energy brushes off on to you, and some of yours, onto them.

If you brushed arms with another person, on a microscopic level, you could say that some of their skin cells transferred to your arm and some of your skin cells transferred to their arm.

This type of interaction is occurring at the level of energy, and in the case of empathy, it's emotional energy that is transferred.

If emotional energy from another person remains in your energetic field, it has the potential to transform into your emotional energetic space and affect you in a physical and mental sense. This means that you have the ability to continue to feel the emotion, long after you've crossed paths with the person originally experiencing it.

Without proper removal of this passing emotional energy, which we refer to as foreign energy, or energy that isn't yours, it can build and compound. Your energetic field can and does continue to hold on to encountered foreign energy until it is released by you.

Without release, days, weeks, months, and years of encountered emotional energy belonging to other people can fill your energetic field. With so much foreign emotional energy, little space remains for your energetic sense of emotional well-being.

Clearing your aura is like taking a daily shower. With daily showers, you remove the grime from each day and go to bed with a clean slate. Without daily showers, the dirt, dust, and grime from each day compounds on itself. It builds and creates a state where layers and layers of grime become so thick that you can't see your skin.

Clearing your aura daily is a practice in removing and releasing foreign emotional energy from your energetic field. It's the first step in managing your empathic and energy sensing abilities.

If your energetic field is in a state of complete saturation of emotional energy from others, how can you,

1.   Be aware of what your own natural emotional state of being looks like?

2.   Gain true awareness of the emotional energy of any present situation?

In other words, if the layer of dirt on your skin is so thick that you haven't seen your actual skin in years, how can you be sure what it looks like normally? How can you be sure when a new piece of dirt or a piece of glitter is added?

In starting each day with a clean slate, you have the knowledge of what it feels like to be in your pure and only you emotional state. In going out into the world, you can be certain when a new speck of dirt arises on your skin, and you can remain vigilant to remove it, if need be.

The practice of clearing and releasing is recommended as a daily practice for an empath, and at the very least, intended for use 4-5 times a week.

You are more sensitive to emotional energy than others. With that ability comes the necessity to release the emotional energy of others from your space, so that you can stop feeling that emotion and return to your own state of emotional well-being as soon as possible.

All individuals can unknowingly transfer energy to and from others through their energy fields. We all have the ability, on some level, to sense these emotional energetic changes; an empath is just far more sensitive to energetic fluctuations and impacts to their emotional state.

Empaths are more likely to feel overwhelmed, anxious, or irritable, in the presence of many individuals and equally as many emotional energy inputs.

Empaths are more likely to hang on to and feel the emotional energy of others, far after the interaction has ceased, especially emotions of lower, denser, and heavier energetic vibration.

Empaths are more receptive to the emotional energy of others, simply by their heightened awareness and ability to perceive it, allowing for an easier transfer of emotional energy.

While these truths have pluses and minuses, the bottom line is that your energetic field as an empath naturally contains bits and pieces of emotional energy transferred to you in your regular interactions.

Removing and clearing it from your energy field regularly is integral to your energetic and emotional well-being.

The process of Clearing and Releasing is two-fold:

> **Step 1.** Imagine your energy field
> **Step 2.** Imagine foreign energy being removed

And that's it. It requires a little visualization and can be done relatively quickly with practice, either through pure visualization alone or through combining visualization with the act of physically rinsing your body with water.

Chapter 5 Exercise.
Clearing and Releasing Foreign Energy

The act of releasing and clearing foreign energy from your aura is much like taking a shower and releasing and clearing dirt and grime attached to your skin. The strategy for doing so is relatively the same in either case. In the case of a physical cleansing, you use soap and water to remove physical particles attached to you. In the case of a cleansing of emotional energy, you visualize water from a shower stream rinsing over your aura and removing all foreign particles, with or without also cleansing physically in the shower.

This means that you can combine the act of physically cleansing your body in the shower while also imagining that the same water is clearing and removing all foreign energy from your physical body.

I recommend that clearing and releasing of the energetic body is completed at the end of each day, after you've settled in for the night and ceased most interactions with others. It can also be done multiple times throughout the day, especially if your day is heavy with human interaction, such as being in large crowds, riding public transportation, shopping in a store, or otherwise.

If you shower at night, this is easy to incorporate into your routine, but it's also equally as easy to do seated in the comfort of a chair.

To start, you'll learn the visualization method for clearing and releasing as performed from a chair, and later, feel free to combine it with the actual physical act of showering.

When you are ready, find a chair in which you can sit comfortably with your feet flat on the floor and your back well supported by the seat. Sit with your feet firmly planted on the floor and close your eyes.

With your eyes closed, begin to relax by taking a few deep breaths. Slowly inhaling and allowing your internal body cavity to fill with air, and then slowly exhaling and releasing all breath from your body. Repeat, slowly inhaling, and slowly exhaling, for a minimum of 3 cycles before moving forward. Once you feel relaxed and ready to move forward, begin to imagine your aura (energy field) surrounding your body. Imagine it as oval in shape, and semi-translucent, surrounding your body on all sides, above you, below you, in front of you and behind you. Inspect and observe your aura.

What color is it?

What does it look like?

How far away does it extend from your body? 2 inches or 6 feet?

Is it smooth or rough in texture?

Is it glowing or more subdued in appearance?

Is it pulsing like a heartbeat or relatively stable?

Notate all aspects of your energetic field. If you have trouble with visualization, ask yourself instead, if your aura could look like anything, what do you think it would look like? Trust that your intuitively selected answer is the actual appearance of your aura.

Now that you have familiarized yourself with the appearance of your aura, it's time to start looking for foreign energy.

With your eyes still closed, begin to imagine your aura, now with the intention of locating and finding all areas that are impacted and affected by emotional energy that does not belong to you. For easier locating, choose to assign this foreign, non-you energy a color, preferably gray or black to provide contrast and easy identification.

Foreign energy as emotional energy can take many forms, it can look like gray dust, tiny pebbles or huge boulders and stakes lodged in your energy field.

Any emotional energy that you have encountered during the day can potentially still exist in your energy field. As your encounters will vary with the emotion, the impact, or the situation itself, so will the energetic footprint left on your aura.

Scan your energy field for all areas of potential emotional energy footprint from another, and imagine what these footprints and signatures look like, and where they could have arisen. Speculate how the foreign energy might look when present in your aura and where it might be located.

When you have a good idea of the location and nature of foreign energy in your aura, it is time to clear and release these particles of foreign and emotional energy from your aura.

Imagine now that above your head is a giant, rain shower shower head. Imagine yourself turning the water on, to a warm, soothing temperature. As the water begins to flow over your body, watch and imagine as each and every particle of foreign energy is released, removed, and cleared from your energetic field. Watch as it is rinsed down into the drain below.

Visualize, watch, and imagine each pebble, rock, stake, and all particles of dust and dirt from all areas of your energetic body being completely and totally rinsed off and washed down the drain. Imagine and allow yourself to stand beneath this energetically cleansing stream of water until your energetic field is completely free and clear of all foreign energy.

When you are ready, imagine yourself turning off the water from the shower above, and stepping out from under the shower head, and into a bright, sunny patch of light. Imagine this sun dries you off and feel the warmth on your body. Continue to imagine yourself standing in this warm, dry, ray of light until you feel completely clean and completely dry.

And that's it, you have just completed the act of clearing and releasing your energetic field from foreign energy. Start by practicing this exercise

3-4 times a week. As you get more comfortable with it, moving away from the written procedure, begin to integrate it more and more and more into your evening ritual until it becomes a daily act.

———

In the beginning, it may take several sessions before you start to notice an effect of this practice. If you're an empath working with years and years of emotional energy stored in your aura, it's going to take some time to break down and rinse through all the layers that may exist. Similar to if you've not had a shower in years, it may take several soaks and bathing sessions to break down all the layers of dirt to become completely clean.

Over time, you will begin to notice a distinct change in your emotional state and attitude after you complete this act. The difference will be most apparent if you complete this exercise after a particularly long day filled with interacting with emotional energy, with an aura heavy with the emotions of others.

Taking an energetic shower is the first step in emotional energy management. It creates a clean slate, each day, wiping you free of any emotional energy not belonging to you and no longer serving you in a beneficial way. It gives you the freedom to no longer feel and experience the emotions of others, allowing you to return to a state of balance within your own emotional well-being.

After you've learned to cleanse yourself energetically, the next step is learning how to maintain clean skin throughout the day.

Now that you're nice and clean, how can you stop brushing up against others during the day to maintain your state of cleanliness for longer? Alternatively, if you suddenly encounter a warm ray of light in the middle of winter, how can you position yourself to benefit from this sun?

From a physical standpoint, you're now deciding what your skin is allowed to touch, and what you'd prefer not to come in contact with you skin. In other words, how can you control who and what your energetic skin, your aura, touches to maintain a state of emotional cleanliness and nourishment.

One way to do this is through managing the distance at which your aura sits from your body, through expanding and contracting your energetic field to suit your needs.

A benefit of having an energetic body, not constrained by physical limits of density and solid state, is that you can control your energetic skin, your aura. You can pull it closer to you, for less interaction and sharing, or you can push it out further away, for more interaction and sharing. You can avoid touching dirt, and you can walk into the warm sunlight if you so choose.

You can expand and contract your energy field, your aura, to sense and feel more emotional energy, or to sense and feel less emotional energy, depending on your desires and needs.

Chapter 6

Aura Expansion and Contraction

The human aura is an energy field, not bound by a physical structure or the properties of a solid state matter. Energy isn't matter; it's the component that causes a change in matter. Your aura is made up of energy that causes changes in physical substances with matter, such as your physical body and mind, and the physical body and mind of others.

An energy field is fluid, dynamic, and always changing. Easily and instantaneously changed and affected by inputs coming from within yourself and from outside of yourself.

Auric changes that arise from within are often the result of internally felt emotional changes that you are aware of and can relatively control. However, inputs to your aura that cause change can also come from external sources, from which you may or may not have a clear awareness of the source.

Your energy field, your aura, sits at some distance away from your physical body. This distance can be as little as 1-2 inches or as much as 6 feet or more. The farther away from your body your aura sits, the bigger your radius for picking up on the emotional energy of others.

The expansion or contraction of your aura determines the extent to which you feel, share, and experience the emotional energy of others. The farther away from you that your energy field sits, the more emotional energy you can sense.

It is your aura that first and foremost interacts with other auras to sense, perceive, and receive information about your world in the form of emotional energy existing in the auras of others. Once received and perceived by your aura and your physical systems, this emotional energy can easily be transformed into a physical feeling and sensation in your system. This physical feeling and sensation of emotion can last for long after the interaction itself if the emotional energy continues to reside in your energy field.

When you pull in and contract your aura, to have it sit very closely to you, you are pulling in your energy field. This is done to decrease the level at which you are actively sensing the emotional energy of others. With your energy field so close to you, other individuals and their auras would also have to come very close to you in order to interact with your energy field in a passing sense. In most cases, this happens much less frequently than, let's say, passing someone who is 8 feet away.

If your aura is close to your body, you're receiving far, far fewer emotional energy inputs than you would if your aura were farther out from your body. If you're only receiving and sensing emotional energy that comes within 2 inches of you, there's going to be a lot less of it to sense during your day. In most cases, you'll be much farther away from others than that.

On the other hand, if your auric radius expands to 6 feet in all directions from your body, you're looking at a diameter of 12 feet across. A 12-foot span in which you are open to receiving, sensing, and perceiving the emotional energy of all those that come within your field. This is a huge span of sensing emotional energy. With an energy field this large, you are now likely going to be receiving emotional energy inputs from many, many more individuals throughout your day. Far more than if you were only sensing emotion from those who came within 2 inches of you.

You can see why having a huge aura might be a problem for someone who is sensitive to the emotional energy of others.

Put simply, the bigger the aura, the more emotional inputs you receive. With a bigger aura, you are more likely to feel low energy emotions (and high energy emotions) and feelings of overwhelm and exhaustion from sensory overload.

Low energy emotions tend to hang around in the aura for longer, because they are heavier, denser, and have a longer vibrational pattern. Even if you did choose to surround yourself with high energy individuals, when you have a large aura, you're encountering, far, far more emotional energy than just those who you allow to get close. And in these encounters, it's extremely likely that you'll run into contact with someone, somewhere that was having a bad day and experiencing a low energy emotion.

There are, however, cases when having an expanded, large aura is beneficial. These are cases in which you wish to share, completely, in the emotions of another person or group of people.

For example, if you've ever been to a wedding where the love and happiness in the room were palpable, this might be a scenario in which you might choose to expand your aura. In doing so, you can feel more fully the love and joy present in each person in attendance.

Community building events, births, joyful rites of passage, birthdays, and other celebratory and love filled events are all potential scenarios in which you may choose to expand your aura. These are events where you may choose to accept willingly into your emotional space all the free flowing, high energy emotion present.

In general, expanding and contracting your aura has two specific purposes:

> **Auric expansion** is used to turn up or increase your empathic abilities, to feel and share in more high energy loving emotions.

> **Auric contraction** is used to turn down or decrease your empathic abilities, to avoid feeling and sharing in the low energy emotions of others.

Auric expansion and contraction are active awareness and prevention techniques that allow you to change your auric distance to suit your needs in preparation for or in response to a specific event.

> *Going to the airport?* You may want to pull in your aura to avoid emotional inputs from anxious travelers.

> *Attending a wedding or engagement ceremony?* You may choose to expand your aura to soak up and be fully present in the energy of love and happiness.

> *Preparing for a stressful work meeting?* Consider pulling in your aura to protect yourself from sharing in the stressed emotional energy present in the meeting room.

> *Watching your child's first dance recital?* Expanding your aura could allow you to

collectively share in the feelings of each parent's love, support, and pride for their child.

In addition to these preemptive examples, you can also expand and contract your aura on the spot. As soon as you gain awareness that a change is needed to maintain or enhance your current emotional state, you can act. You can easily excuse yourself to another room if you need to but with practice, you can learn how to visualize this act without anyone even noticing!

So, if you suddenly find yourself on a crowded bus or at a popular farmer's market, you can easily make auric changes and manage your energetic well-being on the fly.

When you first begin practicing with auric changes, we suggest making auric adjustments in advance of a known situation that you've previously noticed yourself feeling emotionally unwell (Chapter 2 Exercise).

For example, if you get social anxiety and feel nervous amid large groups of people, contract your aura before you even leave the house to attend your next social gathering. This way, you can avoid sensing the emotional energy of all others at the social gathering, which tends to be the source of social anxiety.

On the other hand, if you find yourself having difficulty feeling connected in the moment and sharing in the love present during a wedding, try expanding your aura before you arrive. When you do, do so with the intention to accept and welcome in the love and happiness emotional energy present.

Chapter 6 Exercise.
Auric Expansion and Contraction

Using the same initial technique as the Chapter 5 Exercise, find a comfortable chair in which you can sit with your eyes closed and with your feet flat on the floor.

Begin by allowing yourself to relax, through slowly inhaling and slowly exhaling. Take a few deep breaths, inhaling completely until you feel your lungs filling and stomach expanding, and exhaling completely until all breath has been released from your lungs. Inhale and exhale deeply for at least 3 cycles before moving on.

When you feel ready, begin to imagine your aura, focusing on its distance from you. Imagine and visualize what it looks like, its color, its shape, and how far it extends from your physical body. Take note on how far it currently extends out on all sides surrounding your physical body.

Is it 3 feet away?

Is it 3 inches away?

Is it 5 feet away?

Is it 10-12 inches away?

An aura is considered close to your body, at roughly 6 inches or less and far away at 1 foot or more. Imagine at what distance your aura currently resides. If you struggle with visualization, simply postulate, at what distance your aura resides if you could choose a distance.

For this exercise, choose **Aura Expansion** if your aura is close to you and **Aura Contraction** if your aura is far away.

Aura Expansion

If your aura is close, imagine it slowly pushing outward, expanding to fill a greater distance from you and a further radius surrounding you. As if your aura is a red balloon and it's slowly being filled with air, getting bigger and bigger, imagine your aura expanding to a distance that feels comfortable to you. Is your auric balloon only half inflated, or is it inflated all the way, to near translucency?

This could be 3 feet or 6 feet. Stop when you feel ready to stop. You may have to practice this exercise a few times to find a distance comfortable for you. Expand your aura to fill a certain distance, and then, go about your day and notice the changes and impacts of an aura at that set distance. It may take a few times before you settle on a distance that feels right to you. Some people, prefer a balloon only halfway inflated while others prefer to inflate the balloon until it is almost translucent and ready to pop. It's matter of personal preference and situational factors. With practice, you'll get an idea for which distance feels most comfortable to you in certain situations.

Once you have visualized your aura expanding to the place where you feel comfortable, you're done. You've successfully expanded your energetic field to a distance farther away from you, by thought alone. This is possible because thought carries with it intention and energy, and through energetic transformation has the power to shift your state of being.

Aura Contraction

If in the initial exercise, you imagined or postulated that your aura was a farther distance away from you, practice bringing it in closer. Imagine that your aura is a full balloon that is now slowly deflating, getting smaller and smaller in size and diameter until only a little air remains within. Imagine that this auric balloon is surrounding your physical body, and allow it to deflate until it reaches a point so close to you, almost touching your body, aiming for a distance of 1-2 inches away.

Perhaps you choose to visualize your aura close to your physical body, but not too close, at 3-4 inches away on all sides. From there, you can decide if this closeness creates a harmonic balance between too much and too little sensing of emotional energy.

Once you've imagined your aura contracting to a smaller radius, closely surrounding you on all sides, you're done.

In both auric contraction and expansion, the key is practice. Experiment with a variety of distances close and far away from you in a wide array of situations.

If you're planning a shopping trip to a store that normally makes you anxious and irritable, before you leave, try contracting your aura to a distance close to your body, perhaps 3 inches away. On your trip, take notice of your emotional state and reactivity.

> *Do you feel overstimulated or anxious?*

> *Do you feel centered and balanced?*

> *Do you feel confined and constricted?*

> *What about after you leave, do you feel irritable when you were calm before?*

With answers to these questions, you can adjust your auric distance to perfectly suit your comfort level for future trips.

This exercise gives you the ability to expand and contract your aura to suit your emotional and energetic needs of the situation, your sensitivity level, and your ever fluctuating emotional and energetic state. It's now a matter of fine tuning the positioning of your energetic field for an optimal state of being.

Practice auric expansion and auric contraction, each, at least 2-3 times each week before you start your day or leave the house. Make it your goal to experiment with different contexts, different places, and with different distances. Continue practicing this exercise until you become familiar with how auric expansion and contraction best works for you as a tool for managing your emotional energy sensing ability. Remember to take note of changes, effects, and benefits of managing your aura in several contexts.

> *Do you feel more or less anxious than you normally would?*

> *Do you find yourself having clearer and more compassionate interactions with others?*

> *Do you feel more or less tired and exhausted at the end of the day?*

While you practice, maintain an awareness of your emotional well-being. Each person has a unique degree of sensitivity to emotional energy, a unique acuity to certain emotions in certain situations, and managing your own energy field is highly personalized and tailored to your specific needs.

———

In the management of your energetic field and emotional life, the only way to design your ideal energetic and emotional state is by identifying what that looks like for you. Reaching your balance is a process of tinkering until you find what works for you.

Your desired and ideal closeness of your aura will likely be different depending on the situation. You'll have to make different adjustments if you are going on a trip to the grocery store during off hours than if you were going to a crowded Saturday morning farmer's market.

> *Do you anticipate encountering many people or few?*

Do you anticipate being in the presence of mostly low energy emotion or high energy emotion?

Are you open to experiencing and sharing in the emotion of others, or would you rather mind your own business today?

Consider these questions and others, as you make choices for your own best emotional interest.

For example, many people like to contract their auras in these scenarios:

- In crowded areas like airports or shopping malls
- In areas with the presence of low energy emotions such as nervousness, agitation, anxiety, or sadness, like doctors offices, hospitals, and waiting rooms
- When meeting with individuals that are known carriers of mostly low energy emotion, like your friend that complains a lot.

Alternatively, expansion of the aura is used in situations where you want to:

- Accept and welcome in the energy of others
- Obtain better understanding of another person's situation
- Gain clearer awareness of how you can best support and give your love and compassion to another person
- Increase your receptivity when you are in the presence of joy, love, and happiness, in situations like weddings, joyful rites of passage, birthdays, celebrations, and in daily joys and successes

With experience and practice, this will become such an intuitive and natural process, that you will merely only need to have the thought to adjust the size of your aura, and it happens in an instant. In this way, you'll be able to adjust your auric size in mid-conversation with others and out in public without anyone even knowing that you're doing.

To get to that place, it takes practice.

When you first start driving, you can barely pay attention to the road while also controlling the brakes, steering wheel, and gas pedal, let alone have a conversation at the same time. And now that you've been driving for several years, the act of driving and talking at the same time is so natural and effortless. You rarely find yourself thinking of what the steering wheel is doing while in mid-conversation, you just intuitively guide the wheel in the direction it needs go.

Emotional energy and auric management can be this easy, with a little effort and practice in the beginning. Soon, you'll be contracting your energy field without skipping a beat in conversation.

Auric expansion and contraction and clearing and releasing of emotional energy, are both broad scale, wide spectrum techniques.

However, there are certain situations that can affect your emotional energetic state in the moment, regardless of how close your aura resides or how often you release and clear energy from your aura.

These situations are direct interactions with other people where body language, words, or glances are exchanged. Movement of the body, spoken word, and eye contact are all processes that require energy and enact energetic transformation. They carry with them an emotional energy as well. When these gestures are directed at you, it is as if the emotional energy from another person is thrown directly into your energy space.

Beyond passing encounters and brushing past of other people's energy fields, the direct interaction with other people allows for a direct and active exchange of emotional energy between energetic fields.

Exchanging words, looks, or gestures, are at the same time, exchanges of emotional energy from you to another person and vice versa.

Imagine if someone yells an insult in your direction, on an energetic level, this is their emotional energy in the form of words, being sent in your direction with the intention to affect your emotional energy. It's an active transfer of emotional energy.

Now imagine that you've taken a trip to the store with your young children. In the checkout line, things have devolved into screaming and yelling while you try to hold it together and get out of the store. During this time, you notice that a woman standing 2 people behind you is extending a compassionate, understanding glance and facial expression. Even without exchanging words, she is sending her emotional energy in the form of compassionate body language, to your energetic space. She is directing her emotional intentions to you and creating an energetic bridge between you and her.

This connection allows for a transfer of energy from her energetic field to your energetic field.

In direct and active interactions with others, there is also active and live transfer of emotional energy between individuals. You have the power to break this connection, and stop the transfer of energy before it even has the chance to impact your emotional state. Alternatively, you also have the power to welcome in emotional energy being sent your way if you so choose.

This is known as intentionally accepting and refusing emotional energy. This is proactive, in the moment, emotional energy management. You have the power to make immediate, snapshot decisions, of which emotional energy you choose to refuse and which emotional energy you choose to accept, if any.

Chapter 7

Intentional Acceptance and Refusal

Direct transfer of emotional energy, in your active interactions with others, creates a more specific transfer of emotional energy. In these scenarios, emotional energy is specifically directed at you, either intentionally or unintentionally. This can happen when someone speaks to you, gives praise or gives criticism, glances in your direction, or even so much as has a thought about you.

More than just passing auric interactions, direct interaction sends emotional energy to you specifically. When this happens, the emotional energy first makes contact with your aura and is received and interpreted. Then, it is sent to one of your energetic centers, your chakras, to exact a specific, appropriate emotional, behavioral, and reactive response.

When you directly touch a hot stove burner, the interaction is first received and interpreted by the peripheral receptors on your skin. Then, this information is transmitted to your centralized processing system, your central nervous system, to exact an appropriate response. In this case, the response is one of the motor cortex to move your hand away, and one of activating pain receptors to condition you to avoid such an interaction in the future.

In this direct interaction, your peripheral system of your skin received the information and translated it to your central system for an appropriate response. This exchange also occurs at the level of an energetic transformation in muscle impulses, nerve firings, and receptor activation.

When you directly interact with another human, you create a bridge over which emotional energy and information are exchanged between your energetic bodies.

This is much like linking with another person in a handshake, creating a direct connection from which you can gain information about the other person and they from you.

Once the emotional energy bridge is created, and energy is transferred to you, and you have to actively decide to end the interaction and either send back the emotional energy or allow it to stay.

In a sense, you have to break your handshake and decide if this is someone you'd like to get to know, or if you'd rather just be on your way.

You don't have to welcome and get to know all people that introduce themselves to you and the same is true for emotional energy. You don't have to accept and allow in all emotional energy that is sent to you in the offering of an energetic bridge.

You can decide to accept and welcome in only loving and kind energy, and to refuse at the door any angry and spiteful energy.

This is the idea behind intentional acceptance and refusal of emotional energy, making choices actively in your interactions, on what emotional energy you choose to welcome in and what emotional energy you choose to turn away.

If someone shoots you a judgmental glare, is this judgmental emotional energy something you're willing to accept? If your answer is no, you can refuse it.

If you've having a difficult time, and someone reaches out to offer their love and support, is this loving and supportive emotional energy something that you wish to welcome? If your answer is yes, you can actively choose to accept it.

Depending on the nature of the emotional energy bridge created and the wording of the comment, the intended direction of effect on your emotional energetic system differs.

Recall that each emotion carries with it a specific type of energy, either of low or of high vibration. Low energy emotions generally have an adverse effect on your emotional state, and high energy emotions have a more positive effect on your emotional state.

In order to maintain optimal functioning of your emotional and energetic system, it's important that we do what we can to facilitate optimal energetic state, which is a state of high vibrational energy.

To keep your energetic system functioning fully, optimally, and smoothly, we have to prevent, when we can, other people from throwing low emotional energy logs in the fire.

High vibrational emotional energy is the goal, to primarily reside in a state of peace, of joy, of happiness, and of pleasure. This emotional energetic state is resonant with the overarching goal of humanity and the Universe as a whole. As a collective, we strive to reach a state on the high energy side of the spectrum.

Closer to love, than to fear

Closer to light, than to dark.

Closer to happiness, than to sadness.

The goal of all individuals is to achieve happiness, and in this sense, to achieve a state of high emotional energy.

To reach that state, we have to find within ourselves a place of balance and peace. We also have to find a place of balance and peace outside of ourselves, not allowing the emotional energetic states of others to have lasting impact on our own desire for happiness and high energy emotion.

When you interact with others, you are interacting directly with the emotional energetic state of another person. That person's emotional state has nothing to do with you. They could be experiencing low energy emotion or high energy emotion, just for a single day, or through the period of their lives that you are coming into contact with them.

To reach a place of happiness, love, and joy, you have to be cognizant of the attempts of others to change your emotional energetic state, either intentionally or unintentionally.

As humans, it is our inherent desire to reach out and connect with others and to share our feelings and our experiences, to be heard, seen, and noticed.

When someone extends to you a low energy emotion, realize that it comes from outside of yourself, from another person. An insult in your direction, a glare, a criticism, or a harsh comment, these are low energy emotions generated from another person and sent in your direction. These do not come from you, and it is not your responsibility to share in that that emotion, jeopardizing your energetic state of balance.

A low energy log is being thrown on your fire, and you have the ability to kick the wet log away immediately to prevent the dampening of your fire.

This is called **intentionally refusing emotional energy.**

At the same time, imagine you encounter someone in a state of high energy emotion when they are feeling love, care, happiness, and compassion. If they decide to extend to you a piece of this energy, why not accept this tinder to your fire? It may come in the form of a helping hand, a nice gesture, a compliment, or an understanding look. Accepting high energy emotion is beneficial and allows you to boost your emotional well-being to an even better place, by receiving an addition of high energy. This is a gift and you are welcome to accept it.

This is called **intentionally accepting emotional energy.**

Imagine that you decided to build a campfire. After carefully stoking the fire, and building the flame to a place of stability and warmth, you reach a place where your fire is continually generating high energy. Through this high-energy generation, the fire feeds on itself and is self-sustaining.

Now imagine that a neighboring camper comes to your fire and introduces himself. At the fire's edge, this camper either stands with a bucket of water trickling over your fire or extends a handful of kindling. Either an offering to put out the energy of your fire, and bring it to a place of low energy or offering to add and build to your fire, boosting its already high energy.

In the first scenario, you'd likely tell the camper to hit the road, and you have no interest in allowing him to put out your carefully tended fire. You'd stop the water bucket as it trickles on your fire before it completely dampens the flame, and you remove this person from knocking down your energy level a few or several pegs.

In the second scenario, you'd likely welcome and accept this offering of tinder to further build and stoke the flames of your fire, allowing your high energy fire to receive a boost. You don't have to accept, but most everyone can agree that you can never have too much dry kindling in the event that your fire needs a boost.

You can do this with emotional energy, too, through actively refusing the low energy emotions sent your way while actively accepting the high energy emotions sent your way.

The goal is maintaining energetic balance in favor of high energy emotions, such as happiness, love, joy, elation, and compassion. You want to stay on the high emotional energy end of the spectrum to the greatest extent possible.

If someone sends low emotional energy your way, your empathic ability allows you to naturally and immediately sense, perceive, and feel this emotional energy. Your job is to refuse it and turn it away before it can enact a lasting change in your emotional energetic state.

Likewise, if someone extends a bridge of high energy emotion in your direction, you can choose to accept this energy to boost and enhance your own state of emotional well-being.

The choice is always yours to accept or refuse energy. You can accept low energy emotion, too, if you so desire, and you can choose to refuse high energy emotion sent your direction.

However, it will always remain the recommendation to refuse low energy emotion, and accept high energy emotion, with no strings attached of course.

Your goal as an empath and as a human is to reach a state of happiness and peace. You can get there by aligning your energetic state in a place of high energy, refusing attempts to knock you off your high horse, and accepting offers for a little extra boost along the way.

In the real world, how do you practically accept and refuse energy? In completing the exercise below, you gain the tools to actively make these energetic, snapshot decisions.

Chapter 7 Exercise.
Intentional Acceptance and Refusal

Just as you can actively refuse a wet log or accept kindling to your fire, using your voice and body language, you can use the same technique in refusing or accepting emotional energy into your energetic field.

If someone approached you and offered you a poisonous scorpion, you might put your hands out in front you to block the offering and say, "No, I do not want that scorpion." You are stating that you refuse to accept the scorpion offered to you.

Now, if someone approached you and offered you a piece of cake, you might take it with open arms and say, "Yes, I would love to accept that piece of cake from you." You are stating that you are openly accepting and welcoming of this cake offered to you.

You are using both your voice and body language to accept or refuse a physical offering and you can use these same strategies to accept or refuse an offering of emotional energy.

Intentionally refusing energy

When someone directs towards you a harsh criticism, an insult, a judgmental glare, or a hurtful comment, this is an offering of low emotional energy. This low emotional energy, comes from another person's energetic center, and being extended to connect with your energetic center. An offering of a poisonous scorpion to which you can refuse to accept.

If you would rather not take on the low emotional energy sent your direction by another person, simply state out loud or in your mind that you refuse to accept that emotional energy. At the same time, also extending your hands out of in front of you in the position of blocking an offer, with palms facing out, in front of your body.

Depending on your degree of comfort and your desired level of privacy, this refusal can be as simple as a thought in your mind. As you interact with another person, state in your mind that you refuse to accept this energy.

You can also say it out loud, tactfully, with your words, that while you appreciate their point of view, their comment was hurtful and not needed. This is a vocal rejection of energy.

At the same time, you can also position your hands in front of you, crossing your body, with palms facing out, to block and refuse the energy being sent your direction. This is the body positioning of blocking and refusing. If this action is uncomfortable to you, visualize yourself putting your hands out as a block instead.

All that is required to refuse emotional energy is the decision made to refuse to accept it within your mind and body. How you choose to elucidate this decision after it is made is entirely dependent on your comfort level and desire for firmness and insistence.

The first step in refusing energy is identifying which energy you wish to refuse, and to do that, review the Chapter 2 Exercise in discernment. After you've identified the types of emotional energy that you do not wish to accept, the next step is maintaining awareness of your interactions and refusing to accept any low energy emotion that comes your way.

As you start practicing, it may be the case that you don't realize that emotional energy was sent your direction until reflecting on an interaction after it happens and noticing a change in your emotional state. Even then, you can still reject the emotional energy and kick it out of your energetic space. You can also use the Chapter 5 Exercise to remove this energy.

With practice, you'll learn to catch it earlier, as soon as it happens before it has the chance to adversely impact a change in your emotional well-being.

Not everyone is out there offering poisonous scorpions that you need to swat away to avoid getting stung. Some people are offering energetic flower bouquets and pieces of cake, that you can welcome and accept to feel loved and nourished, boosting your internal feelings of self-love and peace.

Intentionally accepting energy

On the opposite end of the spectrum, are those interactions in which high energy emotion is being sent in your direction. Often, these interactions are equal in number, if not more abundant, than offerings of low energy scorpion emotion. It's just up to you to identify when these offerings of happiness, support, and love are happening so that you can actively accept them.

Sometimes, if you get used to being stung by scorpions and adverse the effects of low energy, it can be hard to open your eyes and see offerings of help in a kind word or a gesture. But these offerings exist, and you are likely someone who does the offering.

The next time someone offers to give you a helping hand, to provide emotional support, or even shares with you an inspirational quote, recognize it as an offering of love, compassion, and happiness. This is an offering of high energy emotion, to which you can accept and allow your emotional and energetic self to be lifted up with the help of another.

Accepting high energy emotion is a lot like accepting help, which many people find difficult to do. In accepting help, there is the acknowledgment that help is needed. Accepting the compassion hidden in the glance of an understanding stranger can be an acknowledgment that in that moment, you are in need of love and compassion. But the truth is, we could all use help, and we could all benefit from a little extra boost of love and happiness.

In accepting an offering of high energy emotion, you're accepting and welcoming in the high energy emotion sent your way by another person. It could be in the form of your sister calling and offering to help with a move or a stranger in line at the coffee shop, turning to you and giving you a compliment.

You're accepting more love, more compassion, more joy, and more happiness. More of this type of your emotional energy in your energetic field, contributes to a more stable emotional state in the direction of high emotional energy, which is what you want, presumably.

You can accept high energy emotion in the same way that you accept a gift offering. In that, you simply state in your mind or out loud, that you are choosing to accept and welcome this energy.

Spoken verbally, you are thanking them and graciously accepting their offering of love or compassion.

At the same time of this acceptance of energy with your words, in your mind or aloud, you can also extend your body language to a more accepting position. Uncross your arms and hold your hands to your sides. This is the position of accepting and welcoming. You may also visualize yourself moving into this body positioning.

Starting with just one day a week, for a block of 3-4 hours, set the intention that you are going to spend that time, paying extra close attention to your interactions with others, being vigilant for offerings of scorpions or offerings of cake. Notice the times when someone sends a low energy emotion your way, and actively refuse it in your mind, with your words, and with your body language, and also notice the times that someone extends high energy emotion in your direction, actively accepting it with your thought, with your words, or with your body language.

You can choose to do this in a face to face setting at your job, while running errands, or while interacting with family and friends, or, you can also choose to do this from a more distant setting, choosing to monitor your phone and internet-based interactions. All interactions have the potential for energy transfer.

Each week, increase your practice time more and more. One extra day, one extra hour, in which you dedicate to actively refusing and rejecting energy.

In the beginning, just like learning to drive a car or ride a bike, you have to give yourself time to remain vigilant while you learn to navigate the world with your new transportation tools. Over time, with more dedicated practice, your ability to navigate shifts from active vigilance to more automatic responses.

Pretty soon, you're identifying emotional energy and actively refusing or accepting it without a second thought. You'll be riding your bike and turning corners, without thinking of which direction to shift your weight.

———

The act of intentionally accepting or refusing emotional energy is an engaged, directed action. At the same time you are interacting in the physical world with another person, you are also interacting on an energetic level. Just as you pay attention to the words you speak and the body language you convey to communicate your emotional needs and desires physically, you must also ensure that the same level of attention happens with your energetically based interactions.

As an empath, it is the energy behind the words and the body language that you feel, it is the energy conveyed in the emotion that you sense. You are sensitive to changes that occur on an energetic scale, below the surface, relatively to the unseen eye. These energetic fluctuations are sensed, perceived, and felt by you in your energetic being.

When an emotion is sent your direction, high or low, good or bad, positive or negative, it has the potential to change and impact your emotional and energetic well-being. It's your job to create and build the ideal emotional life for yourself.

If you don't want to feel or be weighed down by the low energy emotions of others, refuse to accept it into your energy field.

If you want to share and join in the love and joy of high energy emotions, welcome more of it into your life.

In this section, you've learned the essential tools and skills to create the emotional life of your dreams.

Being an empath doesn't mean that you're doomed forever to a life of feeling only the misery of others. It means that if you so choose, you have the ability to feel and share in the full spectrum of emotions present in the human experience.

You can decide what type of energy you feel, when you feel it, and how it affects you.

With this knowledge, you can optimize your empathic gift to use it exactly as you please.

If you wish to use your gift to better understand and counsel others as they move through the grieving processes, you can do that with the full spectrum of energetic and emotional understanding available to you. You can also continue to maintain awareness of your emotional being and acting intentionally to maintain stability in your own energetic field.

If you wish to use your gift to be an amazingly supportive and loving friend, but would rather not feel the emotions of the other farmer's market shoppers, you now have the skills to do that.

With these core tools and foundational knowledge, you can become the master of your energetic and emotional well-being.

As an empath, you have the heightened ability of sensing, receiving, and perceiving emotional energy. You can feel, share, and understand the emotions of others. This enables you to more deeply connect with those around you, through clearer understanding of the human experience, awareness of when love and compassion are needed, and acute sensitivity to a delicate situation.

But, you don't always have to use your gift. Your ability does not always have to be on high alert, and you don't always have to accept everything that is offered to you. You can pick and choose when, how, and what offerings you accept and don't accept.

Your energetic body is your emotional home. You get to choose what emotional energy you allow to enter, when, and under what circumstances as the primary resident. If someone shows up on your doorstep requesting admittance, you can choose to slam the door in their face or welcome them inside with open arms. If a guest arrived with an insult, you would respond differently than if they arrived with a gift. You never have to accept insults – in person or energetically.

You have the heightened and superior ability to sense, perceive, and feel emotional energy at an exceptional rate.

From an evolutionary perspective, this gift is one of the most treasured by village negotiators, communicators, therapists, and healers. With the unique and specialized natural ability to more deeply feel, share, and understand in the emotions of others, you know information without it ever needing to be said. This is considered a psychic ability.

You can shift your behavior and attitude to appropriately respond to any situation, without a single word spoken to you.

You understand and know the exact emotional state of another person, intuitively, without them ever having to explain it to you. This makes you an expert in providing support when support is needed, in lifting a spirit with a smile when happiness is needed, and guarding yourself when protection is needed.

Only now, with densely populated living areas, we're coming into contact with many more people and many more emotions than we were a thousand years ago.

As an empath with a sensitivity to emotional energy, your ability nowadays is often on overdrive. Continually at work to sense, perceive, and make sense of any and all emotional inputs coming within range of your energetic field. Depending on the day, this could be a considerable amount of sensing and perceiving, easily overwhelming your emotional sensing energetic system.

Your gift provides you with a benefit of being able to expertly navigate your environment with your interactions with others. There are times, however, when you may not want to be interpreting and sensing the emotional signals of everyone else and times when your system just needs a break from information overload.

You now have the tools you need to decide when you are actively interpreting emotional information in the form of energy and to what degree, though expanding and contracting your aura. You can now shed days, weeks, or hours worth of emotional energy that is no longer serving to you, through cleansing your aura. And you can now decide which types of emotional energy you wish you share in and also feel, and which types you wish to turn away, through intentionally accepting and refusing emotional energy.

In the following chapters, you will receive directed guidance on which tools are best to use in which settings and situations. There are times when you can prepare for known situations and events, and you can use more preventative tactics. However, there are equally as many, if not more, times in which you need to act in the moment, making snapshot decisions in the best interest of your emotional well-being. You will learn how to manage your emotional and energetic space in a dynamic and unpredictable environment.

You will learn how to apply these tools to a variety of situations, both in preparation for certain known events and interactions, and in the context of on the spot emotional and energetic decisions.

Specific Solutions
for Everyday Use

Chapter 8

Energy Management in Practice

You now have awareness of and practice using the core emotional energetic tools, essential to achieving peace and balance as an empath. The only thing left to do now is to begin practically using those skills and tools in your everyday life.

It's one thing to take classes in master carpentry and to outfit your toolbox with brand new, fancy tools. It's another thing to start taking those skills and tools and putting them to use outside of the classroom, whether professionally or personally.

As an empath, it is not enough to simply know about the energetic foundations and techniques for management. In order see a change in your emotional stability and quality of life, you also have to actively put your knowledge to use.

Even if you took a cooking class to improve your cooking skills, you'd have to take the skills and knowledge outside of the classroom kitchen if you wanted to see changes in your life. You would have to begin implementing your new training and know-how in your personal kitchen to see a change in taste and quality of the meals that you create.

With your new skills and know-how, now it's time to take your empathy management skills out into the real world and use them in practical, everyday, situations.

In using your new tools and integrating them into your life, there are generally two categories of action and directions from which you can choose to manage your emotional energy:

1. *Making preparations in advance of future events*

   Preparing yourself beforehand, or using preparative awareness skills, is a great idea for when you know you are going to be encountering a specific situation and want to energetically and emotionally prepare yourself ahead of time. This is emotional energy management for when you want to do a little prep work to prepare energetically and emotionally for a future event, like feeling joy at a party, or avoiding feeling overwhelmed by a crowd.

2. *Making on the spot decisions in dynamic situations*

   As an individual, interacting with other individuals, most of your energetic and emotional exchanges will be completely unplanned and occur with no future notice. Other people are unpredictable, and it's simply impossible to plan where you'll be and what situation you'll find yourself in at all times. Through trial and error, you learn to react appropriately in most situations and interactions thrown your way. In learning how to make on the spot emotional and energetic decisions to respond to your emotional environment, you can manage your emotional well-being in a dynamic environment.

Emotional energy management is a fluid and changing process. You can prepare yourself for a variety of situations and plan how you might react in those situations, but ultimately, you won't completely know what works best for you until you try.

This section of the book with provide you with situation, emotion, and interaction specific solutions to everyday events. For both preparing for future events and learning on the spot solutions, you will be provided with common examples of potential scenarios. With each scenario, you will find the recommended course of action for handling that scenario energetically to maintain your state of well-being.

Feel free to use the following chapters as a reference area. Flip to each guidance area as you need it, or review potential solutions to situations you may encounter ahead of time so that you have the solutions stored in the back of your mind.

As you begin to put your energetic tools to use, there may come a time when there was an emotional energy transfer, and you didn't realize it until later or did not act immediately. Sometimes we're not paying attention, sometimes we don't want to deal with it, and sometimes it happens so fast that we miss it altogether. You can come back to this section after the fact, and walk yourself through the procedure as if it were still happening, because it likely is, in your energy field. You can also review the recommended steps so that you have the awareness for next time.

Included here you will find the best practice management strategies for the most common situations you will encounter or you can expect to encounter. You will learn what you can do ahead of a known situation to prepare yourself, and what you can do during or after a live interaction.

Chapter 9

Preparative Awareness

As an empath, one of the keys to maintaining emotional balance and stability is preparing your energetic and emotional space before you encounter any potential inputs or change agents.

You can choose to expand and open up your emotional energy sensing abilities with the intention to connect more deeply with those around you, to feel more intimately the emotions of others. Or, you can choose to lock down your emotional energy sensing abilities, to avoid any adverse emotional energy from altering your emotional state, or to prevent feeling exhausted from over-energetic stimulation to your emotional system.

Energetic Opening

Opening yourself up to share, receive, and experience the positive, high emotional energy states is one of the beauties of being an empath. You potentially have the ability to feel an amplified state of love, joy, and happiness just by combining your emotional energy with the emotional energy of another. By accepting and welcoming in the high energy emotional states of others, you receive an uplifting boost to your emotional well-being.

You're more adept and perceptive of the emotional states of others. If you can share and feel joy, love, elation, and happiness simultaneously with others, to a more enhanced degree, why not do it? You receive an emotional energy boost, and by aligning your emotional state with others, you inherently boost the emotional energy level of those around you.

If you know in advance that you are going to be engaging in a situation with a presence of high energy emotions, or you wish to open your heart to another, you can prepare yourself. This way, you can align your energetic state to best experience the accompanying energy boost and connection in these moments.

These types of high emotion energetic events can include:

- **Weddings or Union Ceremonies**
  Associated Emotional Energies: Love, Happiness, Bonding, Appreciation, Closeness, Unity

- **Birthday Celebrations and Joyful Rites of Passage**
  Associated Emotional Energies: Love, Joy, Excitement, Happiness, Pride, Adoration, Amusement

- **Community Building Events**
  Associated Emotional Energies: Sense of Community, Bonding, Connectedness, Unity, Closeness, Friendship, Pride

- **Going on a Date**
  Associated Emotional Energies: Excitement, Adoration, Anticipation, Hope

- **Camping and Outdoor Events**
  (Chapter 5 Exercise)
  Associated Emotional Energies: Relaxation, Peace, Composure, Bonding, Connectedness

Recommended Preparative Steps:

In preparation for these events and others like them, you can decide that you want to arrive at the event ready to experience the emotional energy in the highest and best possible way. To do this and to connect and share in the emotions of others more fully, before arrival, you need to:

- **Clear and release foreign energy from your aura**
  (Chapter 5 Exercise)

- **Expand your energetic field for a wider range of emotional perception**
  (Chapter 6 Exercise)

And you're done! With practice, this can be done in the car or in the bathroom, immediately before you enter the event or situation in which you wish to share in high energy emotion.

For example, you may wish to share in the energy of the wedding ceremony itself, but would rather not open up your aura to the nervous emotional energy existing in the space before the ceremony begins. You can clear, release, and expand your aura sitting right in your chair. And when the ceremony is over, you can pull your aura back in.

In situations where you want to share openly and experience the emotional energy of others, it's best to first clear and release your aura of energy. In doing so, you rid your energetic space of any potential hindrances to a pure and clear emotional exchange. Next, you can expand your aura to the space around you to increase your radius of emotional awareness, and join your energy with others who are experiencing high energy emotion.

On the other end of the spectrum, there are times when you know you'll be entering into areas of chaotic and overwhelming emotional energy, or situations in which the emotional state of being is on the lower end of the spectrum. In these cases, you'll want to adopt a different energetic strategy.

Energetic Closing

Your empathic ability allows you to more clearly and more acutely share, feel, and understand the emotions felt by others, through your ability to sense and perceive emotional energy. Though, there are times when you may not always want to feel, share, and experience the emotional energy experienced by all others. Not only can it be overwhelming and exhausting to always be interpreting, sensing, and perceiving your emotional energetic environment, it may also be the case that you just don't want to accept, share, and feel the low energy emotions of others, such as anxiety, irritation, fear, anger, and sadness.

This is known as turning your abilities down, and manipulating your energy sensing system so that you are aren't so open and welcoming to all incoming energy. You can reign in or close down your energy sensing abilities for the specific intent that you do not wish to receive emotional energy from others.

You can prepare your emotional and energetic state for known events and situations in which you may not want to actively sense energy. Whether you want to avoid overwhelm and overstimulation from excessive energy exposure or to avoid feeling the low energy emotions of others, you can choose to protect yourself.

Events where you may wish to turn down your abilities ahead of time include:

- **Concerts, Crowds, and Taking Public Transport**
  Associated Emotional Energies: All of them. Any emotional energy experienced by any individual in your proximity, leading to overactivation of your emotional sensing system.

- **Shopping**
  Associated Emotional Energies: Weariness, Stress, Confusion, Anxiety, Irritation, Haste. Also See **Concerts and Crowds**

- **Meeting with a Known Negative Nancy or Nancies**
  Associated Emotional Energies: Anger, Frustration, Complaint, Hatred, Despair, Cruelty, Disrespect

- **Commuting During Rush Hour**
  Associated Emotional Energies: Hostility, Irritation, Frustration, Haste, Disrespect, Anger

- **Visiting a Hospital, Medical Office, or Funeral Home**
  Associated Emotional Energies: Worry, Fear, Nervousness, Sadness, Desperation, Confusion, Grief
  Recommended Preparative Steps:

Before you participate in these events or visit such places, you can decide to reel in your energetic field. You can do so with the intention to not take on the emotional energy of others, to prevent overstimulation, exhaustion, and feeling a host of low energy emotions. To do this, before you enter through the doors of the hospital or step onto the bus, you need to:

• **Contract your aura to a point very close, if not touching, your physical body**
(Chapter 6 Exercise)

• **After leaving, clear and release all foreign energy attached to your aura and no longer serving you**
(Chapter 5 Exercise)

The steps for closing are reversed from the steps for opening. The reason is because if you are pulling in and contracting your aura with the intention of having minimal energetic interactions and not feeling any *new* emotional energy, it matters less what is already present, and it matters more that you quickly prevent new emotional inputs. After the interactions are complete, and you've ended the interaction or left the situation, only then, do you immediately need to release any new emotional energy that may have attached.

In a crowded environment or in one where you are surrounded by low energy emotion, you still run the risk of coming into contact with other people's energy. Even with your aura contracted, it's possible to come in contact with energy that you'd rather not have in your energetic space.

It's kind of like checking for ticks. Even if you've made all the necessary precautions, like spraying with bug repellent and wearing long pants, there's still a chance that a tick has latched on and is ready to bite.

In the case of sharing high energy emotions, your risk is much, much lower when the intention was to share high emotional energy in the first place. When you're standing in a pool of sunshine, there are a lot fewer ticks than when you're deep in a dark forest.

With closing yourself off to sensing emotional energy, there's a reason that you made the choice to not feel the emotions of others. By clearing and releasing energy from your aura after the interaction, you are taking the extra step in ensuring that you didn't take on any not-you emotional energy.

These techniques are perfect for preventative care and awareness of *known* emotional and energetic encounters. These techniques are most helpful if you know in *advance* that you're going to be walking into these specific situations and have time to prepare. But of course, most of our interactions throughout the day are not known in advance or predictable, and for these, you need on the spot strategies and follow-up care.

Chapter 10

On the Spot Strategies

Maintaining awareness of emotional energy exchanges, as an empath, is equally as important as staying involved and in the present moment in your spoken, written, and non-verbal exchanges with others. Paying attention to subtle wording and body movements allows you to fully interpret an interaction, as does paying attention to the underlying emotional exchange occurring in all of your connection points throughout the day.

Identifying, throughout the day, when an emotional energy is being exchanged between yourself and another person is only the first piece of the puzzle. Next, you have to decide, as it happens, how much you allow that exchange to affect your emotional well-being. Both steps are integral to creating and maintaining a place of emotional balance.

You are essentially setting up a filtration system, in which you allow only certain energy types of be accepted into your emotional system while all other energy types are not allowed to pass through the filter.

If you've gone to the trouble to secure and purify a water source, you'd want to set up a system that allows only certain elements and molecules to be present in your water source. At the same time, not allowing passage of pathogens and illness causing particles. As your filtering system is fine tuned and optimized, there will, of course, be active monitoring at the point of passage. But, once you have balanced, stabilized, tested and optimized the filtration system, it acts passively without you having to do much upkeep.

With these on the spot strategies, as you use them, you create an energetic filtration system. The more times you allow only high energy emotion to pass and turn away low energy emotion, the more your emotional energetic body becomes aware that this is the system of filtering. Over time, your active emotional management system begins to operate primarily on autopilot.

There will be times where you need to get involved to manage larger and more imminent threats to your filter system, and take a more active role in intentionally accepting or refusing emotional energy. But by and large, by setting up and reinforcing your filtering system through continued intentional emotional management decisions, your system learns. What was once an active process that required full attention, now becomes automatic.

Using an example from the physical world, when you first started to learn to drive a car, you were on high alert at all times. Actively making and thinking about decisions on how to best manipulate the vehicle in a variety of situations. Over time, as you gained an understanding of the vehicle and of the roads, and how they work together, slowly, driving shifted from an active process, to a mostly automatic, non-thinking process. Your body and your mind learned what to do in most situations, only requiring your active attention with major changes to the system, such as when you need to slam on your brakes.

To get to this point, where your emotional energetic system is largely on autopilot, first you have to train it on what you do and do not want to accept into your energetic and emotional space.

You have two choices:

- **To accept and share in the emotional energy experienced by others**

- **To decline and refuse to share in the emotional energy experienced by others**

In most cases, if given the choice, humans enjoy sharing and experiencing high energy emotional states of others, and do not enjoy sharing and experiencing low energy emotional states.

Collectively, we like to feel happiness, joy, pleasure, and love, and we do not like to feel sadness, anger, irritation, and displeasure.

We can actively decide to accept and share in high energy emotion, and to decline and refuse low energy emotion. In making these choices, on a pro-active, daily basis, we are setting up our ideal filtration system. Continually making similar choices, we begin to automatically and naturally make these choices without thinking. Naturally, you begin to gravitate towards a buffered state of emotional stability in high energy emotion, where except for large scale intrusions of low energy emotion, you remain in a stable state of peaceful emotional balance.

Accepting and Sharing Emotional Energy

Actively deciding to accept and share in high energy emotion, such as love, compassion, excitement, joy, and pride in achievement, allows you to receive and experience an energetic boost to your emotional being.

Below you will find a series of examples and situations in which you might choose to openly accept and welcome into your space the high emotional energy sent your way by individuals external to yourself. These are only a sampling of an endless number of exchanges of high energy emotions between individuals.

With each situation and context, you are provided with the types of emotional energies associated with the act, and the recommended energetic steps to take to optimally and fully accept and experience this loving emotional boost.

- **Spontaneous Acts of Kindness and Love**
  When you are the recipient of a spontaneous act of love or kindness, this is a direct energetic link made to you from the other person. To fully benefit and experience the emotional energy transferred in this exchange, accept the goodwill of this loving act and intentionally accept the emotional energy as well. This opens your energetic field and allows you to accept and integrate this high energy emotional act.

  - *Associated Emotional Energies:* Love, Kindness, Appreciation, Respect, Goodwill

  - *Recommended Energetic Sharing Action:* Intentional acceptance of energy, by stating your acceptance of their goodwill out loud, in your mind, and with your body language, as you feel comfortable (Chapter 7 Exercise)

- **Sharing in Achievements and Celebrations**
  When someone you love experiences a major achievement, celebrates a rite of passage, or reaches a goal, you too can experience equally the emotional energy of excitement, joy, pride,

and accomplishment. You can provide your loved one with a sense of support and complete understanding of what this achievement means to them. When your partner comes home from work and announces a raise, or your child opens their first college acceptance letter, you can share in their emotional experience and create a cherished moment of bonding.

- *Associated Emotional Energies:* Excitement, Joy, Pride, Elation, Happiness, Togetherness, Unity, Bonding

- *Recommended Energetic Sharing Action:* Expand your aura, to encompass the person or persons celebrating (Chapter 6 Exercise). If the emotion is directed at you specifically for sharing, also intentionally accept the energy (Chapter 7 Exercise)

- **Gift Giving**
Receiving a physical gift from another person also contains an energetic, emotional gift. Someone else carefully selected a gift with you in mind, considering what types of things you would love, enjoy, and would cultivate the most happiness in you. The gift you receive is one of love, appreciation, and respect. When you accept a physical gift, you can also accept the gift of emotional energy attached to amplify your experience.

  - *Associated Emotional Energies:* Love, Concern, Care, Respect, Appreciation

- *Recommended Energetic Sharing Action:* Intentional acceptance of energy (Chapter 7 Exercise). As you accept the gift with your hands, you already display the welcoming body language, simply add the intentional thought or spoken words of acceptance.

- **Playing, Games, and Laughter**
Laughter evoking happiness falls especially high on the energetic spectrum. In playing games, telling jokes, or watching children play, connecting and sharing in the energy of happiness, joy, and laughter is the ultimate emotional boost.

  - *Associated Emotional Energies:* Happiness, Joy, Elation, Amusement

  - *Recommended Energetic Sharing Action:* Expand your aura to share in the happiness that surrounds you (Chapter 6 Exercise)

- **Expressions of Gratitude**
When you are directly thanked and appreciated for your work, efforts, and contributions, you are the recipient of energetic acknowledgment, respect, honor, and appreciation. This type of emotional energy offering is rare. It is not often, unfortunately, that we are openly and directly thanked, appreciated, and acknowledged for our gifts to the world. When you are offered this type of energy, accept it as an exchange for all your hard efforts. It's a high vibrational offering of great esteem.

- *Associated Emotional Energies:* Appreciation, Gratitude, Respect, Honor

- *Recommended Energetic Sharing Action:* Intentional acceptance of energy (Chapter 7 Exercise), with the affirmation, "I accept the extension of appreciation, acknowledgment, and gratitude for my efforts."

- **Offerings of Help**
  Offerings of help most often arise from other empaths. These are individuals in your life and that you meet in passing, that sense in your energetic field, a need for compassion, for assistance, and for kindness. In interpreting your emotional state, help is offered. Rather than offering from a perception of weakness, another empath offers help because in sharing your emotional state, they decide that in the same situation, it would be nice if help were offered to them. Even if you do not accept physical help, you can accept the emotional energy of kindness and compassion.

  - *Associated Emotional Energies:* Kindness, Compassion, Goodwill

  - *Recommended Energetic Sharing Action:* Intentional acceptance of energy (Chapter 7 Exercise), with the affirmation, "I accept into my emotional space the kindness and compassion of others."

- **Unexpected Compliments**
  Most of us are not used to graciously and openly accepting compliments from others. We

often immediately discount the compliment by stating that we got our outfit on clearance, or that what we accomplished wasn't that difficult after all. To fully accept, emotionally, the love, adoration, and kindness, being showered upon you, it's important to accept all compliments with no immediate discounts. Discounting a compliment can have the energetic effect of immediate refusal of acceptance.

- *Associated Emotional Energies:* Appreciation, Adoration, Love, Kindness

- *Recommended Energetic Sharing Action:* Intentional acceptance of energy (Chapter 7 Exercise), being cognizant to not immediately negate the compliment

In each of these scenarios and more, you have the ability to consciously accept emotional energy from others. These emotions can span the entire high energy emotional spectrum, from love and compassion, to gratitude and kindness, to happiness and elation. By openly sharing, feeling, and sensing these emotional states instigated by others, you accept bits and pieces of that emotional energy. And the more high energy emotion you accept, the more you can shift your emotional well-being to not only stability and balance, but to a state of happiness and love, too.

Allowing high energy emotions to filter into your emotional system has only benefits. You can share, understand, and feel more deeply and sincerely the emotional state of others and the inherently wonderful emotional energy is integrated into your being in the process.

Accepting and sharing in high energy emotion only accounts

for one end of the spectrum of human emotion. At the other end of the spectrum resides low energy emotion, such as anger, nervousness, irritation, spite, hatred, and pain. Under absolutely no circumstances are you required to accept this energy into your emotional system, or allow this type of energy to pass through your filtration system.

Of course, you can acknowledge when low energy emotions exist in others, as you can naturally sense and feel it. However, the line is drawn when you decide to not go any further in sharing the emotional energy. You can still extend love and compassion when it is needed, but you do not need to fully embody and accept their emotional state to do that.

If fact, as an empath, it is recommended that you, to the extent possible, always try to filter out and refuse low energy emotion of others. As a natural energy sensitive, you're especially aware of emotion as it is. On top of that low energy emotion tends to linger as it has more density and slower movement. Low energy emotion, once accepted and integrated into your energy field, tends to stick around for much longer than high energy emotion.

When in doubt, always decline and refuse to accept emotional energy on the lower end of the spectrum.

Declining and Refusing Emotional Energy

In creating your energetic filtrating system, you created a defined framework of what emotional energies are welcome and permitted to pass through to your emotional being. You also need to create a framework of what types of emotional energies are not allowed to pass through the filter.

As an empath and energy sensitive, you may decide that you will not permit anything to enter your energy field that exists at low energy. You can also decide that any chaotic or not presorted energy, as is the case in crowds and public places with many emotional energies present, is not permitted to pass through to your emotional system.

Below you will find a series of common scenarios and situations which are often tied to low or chaotic, unfiltered emotional energy, containing both low and high energy emotions. In these contexts, you are giving the choice to refuse or decline accepting these emotional energies into your energetic space.

With each scenario, you are provided with the emotional context of why you might wish to refuse the energy, the types of emotional energies typically present in the situation, and the recommended best practices for refusing that energy.

- **Arguments**
  Rather than a constructive discussion with civil conversation, an argument filled with spiteful comments, underhanded blows, and lack of compassion is an explosion of low energy emotion. Even in the midst of it, you can refuse to accept and hold onto that energy in your aura and energetic body.

    - *Associated Emotional Energies:* Anger, Frustration, Irritation, Hatred, Confusion, Fear, Insecurity, Cruelty, Pain, and Disrespect

    - *Recommended Energy Refusing Steps:* Intentional energy refusal first (Chapter 7 Exercise), as a broad scale, refusal of all emotional energies in the argument. After intentionally refusing as your immediate response, clear and release remaining low energy from your aura (Chapter 5 Exercise)

- **Irritation and Anxiety**
  Feelings of irritation and anxiety can arise and present themselves primarily in three different ways:

  Option A: Emotional energy externally existing outside of yourself, in your general vicinity

  Option B: Emotional energy originating from someone external to yourself, and specifically directed at you

  Option C: You already feel the emotional sensations of irritation and anxiety from an unknown source.

  In all cases the emotional energy itself is the same, but the management technique differs slightly.

  - *Associated Emotional Energies:* Anxiety, Irritation, Worry, Nervousness

  - *Recommended Energy Refusing Steps:*

    Option A: Contract your aura first (Chapter 6 Exercise), then clear and release foreign energy as soon as possible (Chapter 5 Exercise)

    Option B: Intentional refusal of energy (Chapter 7 Exercise), then clear and release residual foreign energy as soon as possible (Chapter 5 Exercise)

Option C: Clear and release foreign energy as soon as possible (Chapter 5 Exercise), take note of your activities that day, and practice contracting your aura prior to engaging in similar activities in the future (Chapter 6 Exercise)

- **In the Presence of Unhappy Individuals**
You can suddenly find yourself in the presence of individuals that are noticeably unhappy, standing beside an upset shopper, or stuck in a traffic jam with angry and frustrated drivers - it happens all the time. If you do not wish to take on this peripheral, diffuse expression of emotional energy through sensing, receiving, and perceiving you can actively manage your energy field to prevent a transfer and acceptance of energy.

    - *Associated Emotional Energies:* Any low energy emotion, including anger, irritation, frustration, upset, spite, jealousy, or hatred.

    - *Recommended Energy Refusing Steps:* Contract your aura (Chapter 6 Exercise), intentionally refuse any emotional energy directed at you (Chapter 7 Exercise), and then, clear and release residual energy from your aura (Chapter 5 Exercise)

- **Sudden Onset of Sadness**

As an empath, a common issue is the sudden onset of overwhelming sadness and despair, often accompanied by a feeling of heaviness and pressure. If this happens to you, it is mostly likely the case that at some point throughout your day, you encountered someone who was experiencing this strong, low energy emotion without your conscious awareness. Without being aware of it, you may have inadvertently sensed and received this energy in passing, and only now is it being perceived, and integrated into your system, generating a conscious awareness. Even though the interaction is likely long gone, you still hold onto the emotional energy, and you can release it.

- *Associated Emotional Energies:* Sadness, Despair

- *Recommended Energy Refusing Steps:* Intentionally refuse the energy (Chapter 7 Exercise) after the fact. Then, clear and release foreign energy from your aura as soon as possible, expanding your technique to include a more thorough shower (Chapter 5 Exercise).

- **Traumatic Events in the External World**
You can buffer yourself from feeling the full extent of emotional energy attached to a traumatic event in your external world, whether it be a natural disaster, a tragedy, or the painful traumatic experience of another. You can still feel compassion and provide support and caring, without allowing for complete energy transfer and full embodiment of the emotion of those directly affected by the event.

- *Associated Emotional Energies:* Grief, Sadness, Despair, Confusion, and Fear

- *Recommended Energy Refusing Steps:*
  If you are a **support person, and you are a direct recipient of emotional energy**, you'll need to intentionally refuse the emotional energy from transferring to your aura (Chapter 7 Exercise). Then, contract your aura during your interactions with affected individuals (Chapter 6 Exercise), and clear and release foreign energy from your aura as often as needed (Chapter 5 Exercise).

  If you are in the **general vicinity** of events and individuals directly affected, or you are **watching it play out from afar**, the process is the same. You'll need to intentionally refuse the emotional energy that may be transferring to your aura (Chapter 7 Exercise). Then, contract your aura during your exposure to associated emotional energy, (Chapter 6 Exercise), and clear and release foreign energy from your aura as often as needed (Chapter 5 Exercise).

- **Criticism and Insults**
  If you are the recipient of harsh criticism and hurtful insults, from another individual, know that these words are formed from low energy

emotion residing in their emotional being. This energy is unfortunately being sent out and shared with the world through hurtful comments and critique. It has nothing to do with you, and everything to do with the emotional state of the originator. This is why it is essential that you refuse and decline acceptance of this energy before it has a chance to impact your emotional being.

- *Associated Emotional Energies:* Sadness, Fear, Despair, Spite, Hatred, Nervousness, Anxiety, Frustration, Irritation, and more.

- *Recommended Energy Refusing Steps:* Intentionally and immediately refuse the energy, firmly (Chapter 7 Exercise), and clear and release foreign low energy from your aura (Chapter 5 Exercise)

- **Exhaustion**
Unexplained and relentless exhaustion is one of the primary struggles of an empath. Exhaustion occurs when a system has been overworked and under rested. In the case of an empath, this is the system responsible for sensing, feeling, perceiving, and interpreting emotional energy all day long. The more emotional and energetic inputs and interactions you experience throughout the day, without regular upkeep, the more overworked and over stimulated your energetic system becomes. And because your energetic system is in charge of energy for your entire body, an over-stimulation in one area, creates a slowing and tiring of the system as a whole, leading to your exhaustion.

The exhaustion and tiredness experienced by an empath most often occurs when the aura is expanded and accepting of all emotional energy, and when there's a lack of regular system clearing.

- *Associated Emotional Energies:* All. Chaotic energy residing along all areas of the energetic spectrum.

- *Recommended Energy Refusing Steps:* Contract your aura when anticipating exposure to many sources of emotional energy (Chapter 6 Exercise), and develop a practice of regular aura clearing and releasing (Chapter 5 Exercise).

These situations and contexts are only a small sampling of the most common experiences in which you may find yourself confronted with low or chaotic energy emotions. Using these examples, and what you have learned thus far, feel free to extrapolate and extend your knowledge to other situations and scenarios, allowing yourself to make decisions in your own best interest.

In declining and refusing low energy emotion, and accepting and sharing in only high energy emotion, you structure your empathic gift to reach its fullest potential. Primarily experiencing openly the highest and most wonderful of all human emotion, while selectively choosing when and if at all you wish to share and experience the lower energy emotions of others. The choice is yours, and in practicing these tools of on the spot decision making and preparative awareness, you are consciously making choices to craft your emotional experience.

Closing

With active management of your emotional and energetic well-being, you are no longer at the whim of the wild emotional and energetic swings of all those that you encounter. Gone are the days where you were forever doomed to a life of mood disorders and emotional instability.

Refer to this book again and again, as situations arise, to practice and develop your best management strategies, experimenting with what works for you, what doesn't, and to what degree. You can create the perfect emotional management system for your specific empathic gift.

Practice, practice, and practice some more. Apply your skills and tools in as many situations and contexts as possible. The only way to master your emotional environment as an empath is to actively and completely adopt a set of management tools, whatever they may be. What works for you, may not work for another person, and you can only know for sure if you try.

Imagine you completed a cooking class, and then went back to your in home kitchen and used none of the new gadgets you received. You implemented few if any of the new techniques, only to revert to your old cooking style in the comfort of your own kitchen. Can you then say that the class failed to improve your cooking if you weren't actually using the new skills?

Now, let's say you completed your cooking class in Thai cuisine. Then, you went home and outfitted your entire kitchen with Thai ingredients, with traditional Thai cooking tools, and seasonings, and you began practicing your new skills with the intention to create new delicious meals. You could say that now not only did the cooking class help your skills improve, but you helped your skills to improve, too. You experimented and found the seasonings and techniques that worked best for you, and you optimized them to suit your needs.

The Essential Empath provides you with tools and skills that are relatively intangible, and function within the greater framework of the Universe. You now have a deeper, more elemental, and wider perception of the inner workings of your emotional life, from the perspective of the elemental nature of energy.

You have now graduated this cooking class designed to enhance your emotional life. It's now up to you to go home and start practicing the skills and implementing the tools in your own life, in your home kitchen.

Over time, you will need to refer to this book and your notes less and less as you fully integrate the tools and skills learned in this course into your day to day life. You will need the cookbook, less and less.

Soon you will intuitively, and effortlessly, be making choices to manage your emotional well-being without even thinking about it. It will become part of your daily life, your routine, and your behavior. And before you know it, you'll be a master of Thai cuisine, teaching other students all that you know. You'll master your emotional and energetic environment as an empath.

You already have the gift, now is the time to open it up and start using it.

About the Author

Sarah Petruno is a scientifically-trained shaman, writer, and teacher with degrees in Biology and Psychology from the University of Wisconsin-Madison. Using her unique research science based background, Sarah strives to help others understand, and make changes within, their energetic and spiritual lives for their own healing and spiritual growth.

An empath and energy sensitive herself, Sarah struggled for years with anxiety, depression, and mood instability. It was not until she gained understanding, and the ability to manage her empathic gift at the level of energy, that she reached a place of emotional stability and security. Now, drawing on her scientific background, Sarah approaches energetic and shamanic teaching and healing with a practical, methodological, and logical-minded perspective. Visit her website:

www.sarahpetrunoshamanism.com

Made in the USA
San Bernardino, CA
04 May 2016